Highlight Real

Finding Honesty & Recovery
Beyond the Filtered Life

By Emily Lynn Paulson

ISBN-13: 978-1-7338532-1-7 Paperback

ISBN-13: 978-1-7338532-7-9 eBook

Dedication

*To the women who are brave enough
to embrace their truth, and for those who
are gathering the courage to be able to.*

I wish I could show you when you are lonely or in darkness the astonishing light of your own being.

—Hafiz

Table of Contents

Introduction

I open my eyes and immediately wish I hadn't. I can tell by the stark, fluorescent lights above me that I am in a hospital. I don't even need to remember what I've done to know I've made another bad decision. Then again, my life over the last few years has begun to feel like a series of bad decisions. The only problem is that there is an audience watching me, all shaking their heads along the way.

As the voices around me become more distinct, the details begin to emerge: the party, the fight with my husband, the text message saying goodbye, the bottle of pills.

But perhaps more than any bad decision, I remember the feeling, the voices in my head that said, "They'd be better off without you."

They being the audience. My blood, my loves, my husband, Kale, and our five children, who are right now at home with the nanny, being told only that mommy is in the hospital, not that she put herself there.

I come to and begin to wretch. Kale rushes in, and the look on his face once again makes me wish I hadn't woken up.

It isn't a look of anger or frustration. It isn't even pity. It is love.

And I'm just not sure I deserve it. I don't think I ever have.

I turn my head and can't help but think what people would say if they saw us like this: Me lying in a hospital bed, my husband hovering over me crying because I have once again thrown our lives into disarray.

The picture we present to people is so perfectly put together; not a hair is out of place. We show them our highlight reel, but we never show them this: our highlight *real*.

And it is killing us both.

Highlight Real is my story, but as I have come to realize, once I started making good decisions, once I started saving my life, that it is many women's stories.

We live in the picture of the best of us, but we fail to heal our worst.

We fail to heal the traumas that make us, like me, open up a bottle of pills and think Kale and the kids would be better off without me.

We fail to heal the addictions and behaviors and fears that drive us into living lives that aren't really ours.

And for those of us who are married, we fail to heal the big gaping wounds we brought into our marriages, and we're surprised to find that, over time, they have gotten infected. We get sick and we stay sick. As long as the picture looks good, we think we can ignore the illnesses lying just below the surface until, one day, they erupt in the most unimaginable ways.

Most of us have been taught that if we just ignore a problem, it will go away. But that's not how trauma works. That's not how it gets healed.

It is estimated that the human brain has 100 billion neurons, and each of these neurons connects to approximately 1000 other neural networks. The brain fires off over 20 million billion (yes, million billion) calculations per second. If we were to lay out each neuron, we would have approximately 2 million miles of network.

The problem is when someone has experienced trauma, those neural pathways become distorted because trauma breaks the normal processing.

Studies of the brains of human and animal subjects who have been victims of traumatic stress reveal differences in their brains when compared to those who have not. These changes in brain structure and physiology can affect our memory, our ability to learn, and the way we regulate our emotional reactions, social development, and even our moral growth.

The brain is triggered into an intricate flight-or-fight dance in order to protect itself, and we begin to develop maladaptive ways to manage life.

We're not able to exert rational control over things that other people can: things like alcohol, temptation, or our own feelings.

This is why we can never escape unhealed trauma. It drives our behaviors and, of course, our bad decisions.

We end up living in a state of short-term survival: what do I need right now to make me feel better, to make me feel safe?

Unfortunately, when you're working from a trauma state, what makes you "feel" safe rarely provides true safety. That which is beneficial for short-term survival is not necessarily good for long-term health.

Instead, the thing we use for short-term satisfaction—the drink, the cake (or the lack of cake), the flirty text, or the fight with our spouse—ends up bringing us only more dissatisfaction.

It brings us more pain and ultimately causes more trauma, ensuring that the cycle continues... until we end up in a hospital bed, or on the edge of divorce, or simply looking at ourselves in the mirror and wondering who we have become.

I wish I could say that night at the hospital was my wake-up call, but at least I can say it was part of it. It helped me to begin opening the door to change even though the door was heavy, and I was pretty tired by the time I got there.

But once I pushed through, I found something on the other side I would have never anticipated. I found the glorious little miracle that is healing.

I discovered that I didn't have to be defined or guided by my trauma. For many years, I had lived in undefined brokenness, never able to articulate my pain, terrified others would know about it, even as I drowned in its sorrow.

When I finally started to do the work of getting better, I realized that I had to start sharing the broken parts in order to heal.

But first, I had to get real.

Some say that human development, including behavior, is biologically guided. Thankfully, we can take that biology back.

We can begin to connect to something bigger than ourselves and realize that once we are able to get out of ourselves, we start healing from within.

We stop living the role we were assigned and, instead, create our own roles—in our families, at work, in community—that are the best expressions of ourselves.

I will never forget that look on my husband's face, even if I couldn't handle it at the time. He loved that broken woman even in her brokenness. He offered me the love I needed to start showing myself.

I didn't have to judge her or be angry with her, and the world was certainly not better without her.

I just had to look at her the same way Kale did. I had to love her, even the broken parts. In fact, I had to love the broken parts the most.

I had to stop hiding her, thinking if no one knew, she would cease to exist.

I had to share my story, my brokenness. I had to share it not just for me, but so others could heal too.

Once we bring our traumas out to light, once we see how other people can love us through it, we can start to love ourselves a little more.

As Cheryl Strayed once wrote, "The reality is we often become our kindest, most ethical selves only by seeing what it feels like to be a selfish jackass first."

According to most modern neurobiology, the best way to heal a broken neuron is to show it how someone else has healed. Neurons can mirror other neurons, and they can rewire so that when we have a hard day, that glass of wine, piece of cake, or fight with our spouse no longer looks like the answer. It looks like a short-term solution that is not necessarily good for our long-term health.

Instead, we are able to reach out to our community and get real with one another.

We're able to show each other what it's like to wake up in a hospital bed and know you just made the worst decision of your life, yet, still, people are going to love you.

Then we're able to get up and be led out of the trauma and into the healing.

We are able to bring that healing into our homes.

We are able to share the highlights, but also the real.

Chapter One:
Little Big Lies

I watched as the sun flitted through the sprinklers, a rainstorm of sunlight spreading across our backyard. As I lay in the grass, water arched above my head, spraying up into a perfect Montana summer sky. I wished I could be as perfect as that big sky above me.

But I knew I wasn't.

I was eight years old, and I could already tell something was wrong with me.

The thing was, from the outside, everything looked pretty perfect.

We lived in a happy, quiet neighborhood with ranch homes and green lawns and ice cream trucks circling every afternoon during summer days, just like that one under the sprinklers.

My parents met when my mom was only 17, and my dad was 22, set up by their own mothers. My father had already fought in Vietnam when he came back to the States and married my mother in a church in Vegas where he had grown up. By that point, both of their own parents had gotten divorced, and since they were the youngest children in their families, my parents were pretty much on their own.

In so many ways, newlyweds are like pioneers, heading off for unknown territories together, determined to build new lives that might somehow be better than the ones they came from. My parents were no different. After stopping in Helena, Montana on a long road trip for my dad's job, they decided it would be a great place to raise kids, so they moved there right after they married.

We lived there in a three-bedroom home with a green lawn and that lone sprinkler, spraying above my head.

"Emmy?!" my mom called from the house, but I closed my eyes and pretended not to hear her.

"Come in, Em. It's time to practice!"

My parents never pushed me into music. It was just something I happened to be naturally good at, playing the flute the way other people might score in soccer or pick up another language with ease.

Music was my other language, and by the time I was eight, I was already known as a prodigy.

I finally stood up in the backyard, shaking the grass off my Debbie Gibson Electric Youth t-shirt, and headed back into the house to pick up my flute, leaving the magic of our backyard sprinkler behind.

The next day, I would tell everyone that my parents had bought us a Slip-n-Slide, immediately exaggerating our little sprinkler system into something people might envy.

I never understood why I lied. The words would just slip out of my mouth, and by the time they did, it was too late. I would have to own the lie, even if I wished I had never uttered it in the first place.

Psychologists say that pathological lying in children is usually attributed to one of three things: low self-esteem, anxiety, or depression.

Though I didn't understand why, I struggled with all three of those things. Though I had long been praised for being pretty and smart and other kids liked me, though I acted happy and sweet most days, it felt like something inside of me just didn't work right.

I don't know if it was because my family was so isolated in Montana. We were states away from my grandparents who I wouldn't meet for many years. In fact, it wasn't until I was 10 years old that I met my mom's mother; I didn't meet my father's mother until I was 19. I never met either grandfather.

Or maybe it was the way I thought my parents favored me over my older brother. I didn't trust any of it, making me think there was something wrong with all of us. My brother was two years older than me. He paved the way, making mistakes that I became determined, even at a young age, not to repeat.

Or maybe it was just me.

Regardless, by the time I was in elementary school, I was issuing lies that made no sense. Whether it was telling my teacher I had finished my homework when I hadn't or telling the kids at school I had spent the weekend in New York when I'd done no such thing, I lied without really thinking about it.

I was deemed "gifted" by whatever standards were appropriate for a five-year old child at that time and placed into first grade instead of kindergarten, making me well over a year younger than my peers. I was terrified, overwhelmed by the longer days and being separated from my mother. To compensate, I realized that if I lied about being richer, stronger, or more fun—*whatever* the situation called for—somehow the fear didn't take hold. Lies kept my fear at bay.

Many years later, I would learn the term, "Fake it till you make it."

I had to laugh. I had been faking it my whole life.

Later, I realized the lies were there not just to make myself look bigger or better than I was, but to hide who I really was.

"We have a horse too," I said. I was in a small circle of girls at school.

Nicole cocked her head. She owned several horses. "You do?" she asked.

We were in second grade, and most of my classmates had been to my house where there was no evidence of a barn or any animal bigger than a cat.

"Mmmm hmm," I replied nonchalantly, knowing that the vaguer I was, the less people would ask questions. "He looks like yours."

The girls all nodded, and I smiled proudly. "I ride him almost every day."

The bell rang, and we ran back into school. I was proud of myself until I sat down at my desk. It always happened like that. When I would first tell the lie, I would be flooded with pride, like I had just won something, but then, after a few minutes, I would feel terrible guilt. I didn't understand why I would do it. Looking back, a part of me is still confused by it.

I would even tell lies about my musical ability, but to detract from it rather than enhance it. Whenever people asked me how much I practiced, I would tell them "at least two hours a day." But the truth was I really didn't need to practice that much. In fact, I rarely practiced at all. I could perfect a new piece in about 15 minutes, but I was too embarrassed to admit as much. I felt bad about being less than, but I also felt bad about being more than.

As the youngest kid in my class, the smallest, and, in many ways, the most immature, I overcompensated through tall tales to make up for what I lacked in height and age.

As I've learned over the years, it's absolutely normal for people to lie to cover up mistakes, to gain the upper hand, to be polite, and to be mean. Then there are people who lie pathologically, ignoring or disregarding reality. Others lie to themselves, creating a false but comforting self-image.

In 2005, there was a university study that discovered the first proof of structural brain abnormalities amongst people considered to be pathological liars. They found that pathological liars actually had significantly more "white matter" and slightly less "gray matter" than those who were not pathological liars. White matter is usually a sign of greater connectivity in the wires of the brain, meaning liars are able to process information more quickly and, likewise, are able to more quickly concoct, cover up, and carry on with a lie.

As one of the researchers said at the time, "Lying takes a lot of effort. It's almost mind reading. You have to be able to understand the mindset of the other person. You also have to suppress your emotions or regulate them because you don't want to appear nervous. There's quite a lot to do there. You've got to suppress the truth."

I built my whole self-esteem on those lies. I was not only outwitting my friends and my family. I was outwitting myself.

As long as the picture of what I was presenting looked good on the outside, it didn't matter that I didn't feel good or right on the inside.

I learned by the time I went into fifth grade how to draw a pretty picture for people—one in which I owned a horse and six cats (we had two) and had to work extremely hard to learn an instrument I played with ease.

I created my own reality in which the sprinkler in my backyard became a Slip-n-Slide, and I was confident in myself.

In turn, the other kids liked me. All of them. From the sweet to the popular to the bad kids in school. I was friends with two of the toughest girls in my school. They would walk around the block and smoke cigarettes in our neighborhood, something I had no desire to do.

"You wanna come with us, Emmy?" Jess asked me, standing there in a cut-off Poison t-shirt, her bangs thick and high with hairspray.

"Sure," I shrugged as Jessica and April lit cigarettes, offering me one before we started walking. I said no, but it didn't matter. All that mattered was that Jessica and April liked me. They certainly didn't like everyone.

I'm not sure if my lies allowed me to fit in everywhere, but by the time I was 10, I was a chameleon. I could be friends with the popular kids, the unpopular kids, and now, even the bad kids. Jessica and April didn't care that I didn't smoke cigarettes or use swear words like they did. They accepted me, even though I hadn't accepted myself.

Later, I would hear the term "hole in the soul," but I didn't understand what my soul was when I was in elementary school. Souls can be pretty mysterious business, and it would take me nearly 30 more years to get to know mine. All I knew was that there was something missing, and I tried my best to find ways to fill it.

With friends. With my music. With all those lies.

They were all little big lies—things that were absolutely false but didn't seem to matter much. They were things no one else would care about but me.

As Mary Oliver once wrote, "And now I understand something so frightening & wonderful—how the mind clings to the road it knows, rushing through crossroads, sticking like lint to the familiar."

By the time I was 11, and in the seventh grade, those lies paved the road of my life.

The more I tried to look good in the eyes of other kids, the worse I felt about myself. Instead of gaining more self-esteem, I just started to feel worse. The emptiness and loneliness and anxiety grew. Now I wasn't just different; I was weird.

And there was no worse thing to be in junior high than weird.

I started lying to look "cool," but then I lied just to cover the lie. I had to keep track of all of my untruths, and it felt like every day at school was a landmine of stories I'd told people, sometimes recklessly, about a life that wasn't actually mine.

I was no different at home.

"How was school today?" my mom would ask.

No matter how lousy it was, I would answer, "Good, Mom."

I would sometimes even add in a story about how much fun I had or some cool thing we hadn't actually done.

My parents didn't have much of a social life. My dad would invite some guy friends over once in a while. I only remember one or two women who my mom called friends. My brother and I and our small house in our small town was their world, and that was fine with us.

My childhood was happy but not extravagant. An outing in our house meant a trip to the store. I mean, we still did fun things like camping or vacationing in Canada (because it was close by and we could drive there), but we didn't have the means to do everything. We didn't ski or golf because those were expensive things, but we made cookies and always went ice skating at Christmas. We never felt like we missed out or needed more.

Still, even though mine was a quiet household, happy and simple, I didn't trust it. I didn't trust anything. I didn't trust my family with my feelings, so I felt it was safer to hide them. It was better to tell them a lie about what I had done rather than a truth about how I felt.

I remember lying in bed at night talking with my mom, crying about how seventh grade was so hard. I remember the pain to this day, but I couldn't articulate exactly what it was. Yes, it was hard fitting in. Yes, it was hard being younger and less mature than my peers. But it was so much more. My mom chalked my tears up to pre-pubescent mood swings and did her part to console me. It wasn't her fault that I never gave her real feelings to console.

Sadly, when something finally did happen, when a truth so big erupted in the middle of my childhood, I had already trained myself not to share it.

I lived in secrets long before I ended up with the biggest secret. By that point, I knew how to keep it. I knew how to sweep my feelings under the rug and act like everything was fine.

I was just about to turn 12 and had been doing that all my life.

Chapter Two:
Broken Childhood

I'm pretty sure everyone has that moment, though it probably looks different for all of us. The one defining point in time where we cross over from childhood and into the confusing world of adults. We go from innocence into a dark adolescence with the knowledge that the world can be cruel, that life isn't always fair.

My moment happened on a hot, summer afternoon at music camp. I loved music. It was my happy place. Maybe because I didn't need to talk, my talent overshadowing any immaturity and awkwardness. I couldn't lie behind the flute; I felt absolutely safe there. Sure, you could embellish through dynamics and beautiful tone. You could make the experience better and happier and more meaningful. But you couldn't fake it. Whether the listener knew the piece you were playing or not, it was untampered beauty. Music was pure, and I felt pure when I played.

Which is why I also loved music camp. It was a special annual music festival in Montana for which we had to audition, and though my parents could afford it, it definitely wasn't free. In fact, it was a pretty big financial commitment. It was for the best young musicians in the region, and I was proud to be there.

I was 12 years old, and though I had a three-day "boyfriend" in fifth grade with whom I held hands and a week-long "boyfriend" in seventh grade who I awkwardly kissed after a school dance once, I really didn't understand any of it. I was still at the stage where "going out" with a classmate meant not actually going anywhere.

Of course, my mom had the awkward sex talk with me, but it wasn't anywhere near my little life. Though I was friends with the bad girls who smoked in fifth grade and a couple of girls in seventh grade had "gone all the way," or were at least rounding the bases toward home, I was, for lack of a better word, a prude.

I was totally naïve about the world of sex.

It was my second summer at music camp, and I looked forward to seeing my friends from the summer before. Kids came from all over. We were all pretty good kids—the kind who went away for music camp every summer—and though we might have had "crushes," not much happened for any of us beyond kissing.

That summer, though, there was someone new there, Evan the camp counselor. We had never seen him before. He might have been 18; he might have been 28. I don't even know if his name was really Evan.

Sometimes I wonder where he is today. I imagine he is a married father of three, living in the suburbs, driving into the city every day to work in a corporate

office and heading home each night to coach baseball and pay the mortgage. Or maybe he's some slea-
zier version of the boy we all had a crush on, cruis-
ing down dirty streets until he catches a glimpse of
a girl who looks younger than her age and is willing
to crawl into his car for a $20 bill.

Sometimes I imagine him dead.

Sometimes I imagine being the one who kills
him.

But that summer, he was just the tall, hot counselor
we all whispered about as he led one of the boys'
groups from one activity to the next.

Everything changed one afternoon when we were
walking back from a picnic. I don't know how I suddenly found myself alone, standing in a wooded
area with Evan.

I don't know what about me made me an easy
target. Maybe I wasn't the only girl Evan targeted.
Maybe I was just the girl that day.

Either way, suddenly, there we were, alone in
the woods together. I might have otherwise been excited or nervous, but I knew right away that something was wrong. I was scared.

"We should go find the group," I started to tell
him, but he moved too fast. He pushed me so hard
to the ground that I hit the back of my head. All I
could see was the bright light of the sun as Evan lay
down on top of me.

I don't remember the details. Few people do.

Trauma has a way of protecting us from our
worst moments, wrapping itself like a cocoon

around our memories so that all we know is that when we were 12 years old, a man twice our age pinned us to the ground, ripped off our clothes, and did what he wanted.

I remember not being able to breathe because of the heavy weight of his body. I remember the searing pain as if I was being ripped apart.

I knew what was happening. I was being raped.

I felt like I was there for hours. Now I know it was probably only a matter of minutes.

Evan stood up as I lay there on the ground, stunned, gasping for air, unsure of what I was supposed to do. His shadow blocked out the sun. "Don't tell anyone," he hissed. "Understand?"

I finally got up and tried to arrange my clothes as best I could. All I kept thinking was, *How did people not notice we were gone? Why didn't anyone come looking for me? Why did this happen?*

I don't know if Evan walked me back to my cabin or if I walked by myself.

I got back to my room and took a long, hot shower. I remember how much it stung. I watched water swirl down the drain, stained pink from my blood as it washed away.

I had a lump on my head from where he threw me to the ground.

I always thought when I lost my virginity, I would be much older. I thought I would be in love.

I never imagined this would happen to me.

I didn't cry. I just tried to pull myself together.

A part of me wanted to say something, but I was too scared. Scared of Evan. Scared of what people would say. I was 12. Who was I going to tell? My other 12-year-old friends?

My mom had packed me a package of maxi pads in case I started my period at camp (I hadn't even started my period yet), so I put one in a clean pair of underwear, determined not to let anyone know what happened. I wrapped the evidence comprised of my old underwear in an empty fast food bag and threw it away in an outside trash can. I remember being very aware that I didn't want it anywhere around. I examined myself for other cuts and bruises so I could be sure to have stories for how they got there. I was already well versed in making up stories. I went to bed before my roommate came back and pretended to be asleep though I didn't sleep for a second that night.

The next day was the final day of camp. All the families were coming to watch our big performance before driving us home. My mom and brother came that day. I saw them before our concert, and when my mom hugged me, I burst into tears. There was a part of me that so badly wanted to tell her, but the words just wouldn't come out. I kept thinking, *I can't say it. It will kill her.* We weren't that kind of family anyway. We didn't talk about those kinds of things. I didn't want to cause trouble.

I told her I was just tired, which was partially true. I had never been so exhausted in my life.

I went onstage to perform and got every note right. I didn't care at all.

Music had lost its joy. It was no longer pure. Neither was I.

That day, as we drove home, we encountered a terrible rainstorm. I remember my mom pulling over as I watched the rain pelt the windows. I felt like a different person than the girl who had been driven to camp two weeks before. It felt like there was a terrible, fuzzy gulf between me and the rest of the world. Even as we pulled over and waited out the storm, my mom made a joke about the rain. I could barely hear her. I just looked out into the grey skies, wondering if I would ever be okay again.

I don't remember much else from that summer. In fact, it took a lot just to remember the other details of that time. As I discovered through EMDR, we block the details of our tragedies because our bodies can't process everything at once.

EMDR is a specialized procedure for resolving trauma or lost memories where a client concentrates on the worst moment of their memory while visually following the therapist's moving fingers, listening to a sound bouncing from ear to ear in headphones or holding pulsating orbs that provide bilateral stimulation. You repeat the process until you are able to move through the memory without experiencing any distress. In the process, you also unlock the memories that have been hiding in your psyche since that moment when you hit the ground and everything changed.

It's only been in the last couple of decades that science has truly begun to understand the profound effect trauma has on our brains. It has been discovered that victims may remember exactly what was happening just before and after the trauma, but will likely have a very fragmented memory of what happened during the event. That's due to the way traumatic experiences affect our brain's functioning.

First, when humans are in a high state of fear or stress, our prefrontal cortex becomes impaired or shuts down completely. That's the part of our brain that processes language, allows us to read, and performs high-executive functioning. Basically, our smart brain goes offline. Most of us have probably had the experience of being suddenly confronted by an emergency, one that demands clear thinking, only to find that right when we need our brains to work best, they fail us.

Usually, at some point, fear kicks in. When it does, the prefrontal cortex moves to the back seat, and the amygdala takes control. That's the fight, flight, or freeze system, which will make us keenly aware of one moment but frozen in another. We end up paying attention in fragments, and we only remember some of those shards.

Trauma also affects the third major area of our brain, the hippocampus, which processes short-term experiences and turns them into long-term memories. When we are in a space of heightened fear, the hippocampus has trouble performing that transformation, which is why, all these years later, I still don't remember that walk back to my cabin.

Once I got home from camp, I could barely remember any of it. I just knew I was attacked and I felt utterly alone. Now, sadly, I know that wasn't the case.

There are more than 42 million survivors of sexual abuse in America, and, horrifically, one in three girls are sexually abused before the age of 18. What's even worse, according to the National Sex Offender Registry, "A typical pedophile will commit 117 sexual crimes in a lifetime." There is a good chance I wasn't the only girl who went home from camp that summer a different person. The children most vulnerable are girls between the ages of seven and 13. The fact that we knew Evan made it that much more common. Ninety percent of child sexual abuse victims know the perpetrator in some way.

When I got home, I thought about telling my mom. I thought about it often. But then, one day, she came into my room with a disappointed look on her face. I could tell I had done something wrong before she even told me. "I got a call from camp today," she said.

I sucked in my breath, ready for her to tell me they knew what happened. Instead, she said that the camp had sent us a bill because some of us kids had written our names in wet cement and they had to fix it. My name had been one of them.

I knew right then I couldn't tell her about Evan. Look how upset she had gotten about the cement. At least that's how I rationalized it.

I didn't audition for camp the next year. Music never meant the same thing to me after that summer. Sure, I still played the flute, but it was just something I did, and I had become incredibly skilled at going through the motions. That's what it felt like I did throughout my eighth-grade year and into high school. I acted like everything was normal, and, on the outside, it usually looked that way. On the inside, however, I lost something that sunny day in the middle of the woods.

It took me decades to get it back.

Chapter Three: High School Trauma

"Oh my God, Emmy!? What happened to you?" Meredith stood in front of me, her mouth nearly hitting the floor.

She wasn't the only one asking me that question my Freshman year.

The summer before high school, I hit some major milestones: I went through puberty, took my first plane ride, and went to Disney World—in that order. By the time I came back from the happiest place on earth, I looked like a different person.

Puberty had given me a makeover practically overnight. Growing up, I had always been considered pretty, but people didn't go out of their way to gawk. Once I got to high school, all of that changed.

I had perky boobs, long hair, and great skin. When I walked down the hall, I couldn't help but notice the way boys continued to look at me as I passed them by.

I liked it. I had always been well-liked; now I was the "hot" girl.

"I don't know," I shrugged innocently as Meredith leaned against my locker. "Growth spurt, I guess!"

"You should try out for cheerleading. I'm gonna do it," she said, raising her eyebrows like it was some big secret.

Now, cheerleading might be something most girls in high school did, but I had been more of the band camp type until that point. I wasn't one of those girls, was I? Now, apparently, I was.

I agreed and joined the cheerleading squad.

For the first time in my life, I cared about what I looked like. I curled my hair before school, put on makeup, and wore clothes that looked good on my new body. I also started getting on my mother's scale to make sure the number wasn't going up at all.

Back in sixth grade, at an annual weigh-in by the school nurse, the nurse mentioned that I hadn't grown in height from the previous year and had lost five pounds. She thought nothing of it, and neither did I.

However, when I mentioned it to a classmate, I was met with congratulations.

"Good job, Emmy!" Andrea said, gleaming with pride and grabbing my shoulders.

Good job? Why was that good? That's when it dawned on me: the lower the number on the scale, the happier you would be.

As a freshman, I began to understand the thrill you get when watching that number go down.

Though my social life was picking up speed, and I was turning heads, I was still so innocent. I hadn't taken that first drink. I still hadn't had anything close to normal sex. But those lies from my childhood began to turn themselves into behaviors in my adolescence.

Then it happened. I got drunk. I was 14. A sophomore in high school.

I don't remember the first time being different from all the times that followed. We would drink beers and go to a field to watch planes fly overhead. Immediately, I felt better. All the fear, the lies, even that number on the scale that began to mean so much to me seemed to disappear when I was drinking.

I would lie in the grass with my friends and would be so happy. I'd feel euphoric.

I knew my other friends were having fun, but I could tell it was different for me. I didn't just feel happy; I felt saved. I felt an escape from who I was, like this was who I was always meant to be.

Some of my friends smoked pot, but that wasn't my thing. I just liked drinking beer and staring up at the planes, imagining that, one day, I would fly away too.

It didn't take me long to start dating. My first boyfriend was named Mike. Mike was a sweet kid who really just wanted to play football and lose his virginity.

I didn't want to pretend I was a virgin, and, honestly, I thought he would be able to tell, so I made up a story.

"There was this kid; he went to another school," I began to tell him.

"You already did it with him?" Mike asked me, acting a little surprised but not too concerned.

"No, I mean. Yes. I guess. I didn't want to, but I didn't say no, either." I tried to make it sound like date rape. I didn't want Mike to think he had to play hero or tell someone about it.

My story was good enough to make him feel sorry for me but not enough to motivate him to find some fictional guy at a school across town and beat him up.

We started having sex, but as I realized many years later, I wasn't sober a single time. In fact, I had to drink in order to be intimate with anyone. Sadly, that lasted well into my marriage.

Studies have shown that victims of childhood sexual and physical abuse are six times more likely to drink heavily than their peers. In addition, women are more likely to drink as a result of sexual violence than men.

I didn't realize it at the time, but there was no way I could be present during sex. In fact, it was hard for me to be present...*ever*.

As long as I was focused on my friends or my boyfriend or drinking or what I looked like, I didn't have to think about anything else. I had been such a smart kid, excelling at school and music; now, I was just like every other girl in high school, consumed by hairspray and makeup and friends and parties. And I liked it. I liked blending in.

Though I still played music, I didn't really care about it. I just showed up because it was too hard to explain to my parents why I wanted to quit.

I didn't really care about my boyfriend either. Mike was nice, but there was no connection. It wasn't his fault. As I would find out, I had a hard time making connections in relationships in general. Sex wasn't about intimacy; it was about control. If I was the one calling the shots, nothing bad could happen to me. I felt powerful in a situation I had once been made to feel powerless.

As sex educator Emily Nagoski writes in *Come as You Are*, "Sometimes, too, survivors find themselves locked in a pattern of sexual behavior. Their brains become compulsive about undoing the trauma, redoing it differently, or simply understanding it. Like biting on a sore or squeezing a pimple, the brain can't leave the trauma alone."

Of course, at the time, I had no such understanding of my behaviors. Over the course of the next two decades, I would act out, confused by my decision making, unable to see the lines that always drew themselves back to that day at camp.

The summer before my junior year, I ended up one night at a party without Mike. I had been drinking, and I started flirting with this other guy from our school. We went to one of the bedrooms upstairs to hook up, and, by Monday morning, everyone at school knew about it.

I don't know if Mike was broken-hearted or if his ego was bruised, but he dumped me by Tuesday. I was fine with it. I didn't feel much emotion about anything.

The week before, I had been Emmy. Now, I was a cheater, and there is no brighter scarlet letter than the one you wear in high school. Up until that point in my life, anyway.

In addition to guys watching me as I walked down the hall, now I also heard people whispering after me. Their words lingering long after they were gone. Cheater. Bitch. Slut.

The dramas of high school became the traumas. It felt like there was so little I could control, including myself. The one thing I still had some power over, however, was that number on the scale. I would starve myself, sometimes feeding my dinner to my dog without my parents knowing. If I did lose control, I discovered I could eat as much as I wanted as long as I purged right after.

Starving or binging and purging became my new music. Like with music before, controlling my weight was the only time I could feel pure. I could empty myself of everything, and, for that moment—once I'd washed my mouth and brushed my teeth—feel back in control. I was able to escape.

School was a different story.

All of a sudden, I was like a lonely island. Though I was still a cheerleader, still dated, had friends, and was very social, I knew the majority of people were only nice to my face. That's what I believed, anyway. I would hear people laughing, and I always thought it was about me.

The thing is, the more you isolate someone, the more antisocial they become.

According to a study done in 2015, prolonged loneliness can transform the brain to make it less able to relate to others. Researchers found that animals who were kept in isolation for long periods produced less myelin, the fatty material around neurons that helps them to properly signal. When neurons have issues signaling, they are less able to mirror the networks of the people around them. As the study found, the less mice were allowed to interact with other mice, the less interested they become in interacting with those mice when they actually had the opportunity.

I became one of those mice.

I figured if I was going to be a social pariah, I might as well run with it. Instead of the good girl known for her academics or her musical ability, I started getting a different kind of reputation. My junior year was fueled by alcohol and sex. I would hook up with random guys at parties. I would hook up with friend's boyfriends. Even when I had a boyfriend, I would still hook up with other guys. I would stay the night with one of my friends specifically to hook up with her brother in the middle of the night. I would sneak out my window at night and get picked up by the guy-of-the-moment. I had no guilt about it. I didn't feel particularly connected or interested. All I knew was that when I was alone with a guy, I felt powerful. I was charged by the thrill and excitement of doing things I shouldn't be doing.

Just as with lies, I became a collector of secrets.

Of course, by the end of my junior year, the name-calling only worsened, but a large part of me just didn't care. In a way, the things other people thought about me only reflected the things I thought about myself. That I was a cheater, a bitch, a slut.

By the time I was 16, I started smoking pot and was drinking…a lot. Most of my Friday nights were spent drinking and getting high with friends, ending the night at Taco Bell where I'd throw up in the restaurant bathroom.

You may be asking, "Where the hell were your parents?"

As anyone who partied in high school can tell you, a parent's control is only as strong as their knowledge. My parents were doing their job, but I was doing mine too.

I was a chameleon at school as well as at home. My parents gave me a strict curfew and did their due diligence to keep me out of trouble, but if I told them I was staying the night at Meredith's house, I was off the hook. And if I wasn't at a friend's house, I was sneaking out my window. I didn't have consequences like bad grades or suspensions that would have signaled to my parents something was wrong. Plus, I had my brother's footsteps to follow. Though he wasn't super social, he would get into trouble for not turning in homework. Despite the fact that he's the kind of genius who could ace classes and tests without even trying, the school would still call my parents. They were so focused on disciplining him that, so long as I didn't give them any reasons to look my way, I could camouflage my bad behaviors.

I could make excuses or lie to cover up anything else they might have been concerned about. They only knew what they saw, and they only saw what I let them see.

When people talk about demoralization, I always remember that those were the good times. Those were the years when drinking was innocent. At certain points in my life, I would look back on those days with a laugh. Just kids being kids, right?

Now that I have kids, I don't look at it that way anymore.

I was dying on the inside, but I was so made up on the outside that no one knew.

Finally, I reached my senior year, and, for reasons unknown, started to pump the brakes. I was tired of the names and the bad behavior. Maybe I figured it was my last year in high school, and I didn't want to be ashamed about it. I was only 16 and was already realizing that I needed to slow down.

I ended up dating a really nice guy from school. Craig was handsome, sweet, solid, funny, and well liked. In fact, when I met my husband, Kale, he reminded me a lot of Craig. Someone I could trust. Someone I wanted to care about. Someone I didn't want to hurt, and, that whole last year in high school, I didn't. That was a record up to that point.

Kids can be forgiving just as quickly as they can be cruel. For that final year, I went back to being the Emmy most of my classmates grew up with. My grades were good, I still played the flute, and I was happy and social. I drank, but I somehow managed not to make a fool of myself or end up in bed with someone else's boyfriend.

The only bad habit that carried over into my year of "being good" was my issue with food. At the time, I couldn't even call it what it was: bulimia. It was just a little game I played. It was infrequent, and I was doing so much better. What was the harm?

We were all getting ready to graduate and go to college, and I was looking forward to it. As I was about to quickly discover, nothing made me as hopeful as a fresh start. As I was also about to discover, what mattered even more was what you do with it.

Chapter Four:
A Fresh Start

I arrived at my university dorm room with my cinder blocks and microwave, determined to do it differently this time. I moved to a college just two hours away. I was 17, and when I said goodbye to my parents, I knew I was on my way to becoming an adult.

At first, it felt like I knew what I was doing.

I always excelled at school, and college was like high school on steroids. I was interested in going into science or medicine, so my schedule resembled that of a pre-med student. Biology, chemistry and math. After spending a lot of high school not paying attention in class yet still doing well, I showed up to class early with my pen hovering over my notepad, taking notes, and raising my hand. It was nice to be excited about school again.

In a way, high school began to feel like one big reaction to what happened to me when I was 12; in college, all of that felt really far away. I was free not just from what I did in high school but what had happened before.

College was my big do-over until my do-over started to turn into, oh no…not this again.

Craig was attending a college on the other side of the state, and, slowly, I started going out again. Frat parties, bars that didn't card, late nights, and so many new guys. I felt like a kid in a candy store. It was at one of those late-night parties that I ran into a guy I knew. I guess I had too much to drink, or I just didn't think about Craig. Craig wasn't there, and the old pattern was starting to repeat. Once someone was out of sight, for me, they were out of mind.

Jordan and I hooked up that night though I don't remember much of it. I felt like I was 12 again. Frozen. Unable to stop it. Unable to say a word. I blacked out most of it.

I woke up a few hours later in his bed, knowing we'd had sex, and feeling so much shame I started to cry. He asked me what was wrong. Though I didn't answer, I'm sure he assumed it was guilt from having cheated on my boyfriend of whom he was very much aware. That wasn't it. I was crying because I felt totally helpless. I might as well have been squirming beneath Evan on the ground at music camp.

I must have said yes, but had I been sober, it would have been a no. Does that make it wrong? He was drinking too, so how could he know what I wanted or didn't want? Why would he have pursued me if I didn't seem interested? So many sexual encounters in college are born from this binge drinking environment; a "no" becomes a "yes" because of alcohol. But if you don't remember, how could you have given consent? What if he was too drunk to be able to tell how drunk I was? And how can you tell intoxication versus incapacitation? None of these questions had easy answers.

I walked back to my dorm as the sun was rising, wondering why I felt so sick about what had just happened. As luck would have it, I ran into my friend, Teresa. Teresa and I had known each other since middle school, and though she also knew me when I was busy making a name for myself (her boyfriend was one of my many conquests in high school), we had gotten close again over the past year when I went back to being someone people could trust.

She saw me visibly upset and asked if I was okay.

I shook my head no, convoluting my past with what had happened just hours earlier.

"I didn't want to," I told her, repeating the same story I told Mike years before. "I didn't say no, but I didn't say yes."

Teresa's eyes grew big, "He *raped* you?"

I could have said no. I should have said no. Instead, I just nodded yes.

No one knew about what happened at music camp. She didn't understand that I was having a belated response to a traumatic event. The last person to understand this was me.

All I knew was that I had done something I shouldn't have, I remembered very little of it, and it seemed so much easier to agree to her suggestion. It was easier to say it wasn't my fault than to face the reality that I was the problem.

I wanted my do-over even if I was already doing it again.

Teresa convinced me to tell Craig. Craig convinced me to tell his mom, and I repeated the same story to them that I had to Teresa, mirroring the one I had told Mike in high school.

Unable to admit to the real rape, I created a fictionalized version of it. One where I didn't say yes, but I didn't say no either.

Craig was upset for me and, understandably, wanted to beat the shit out of the guy. His mom wanted me to report it. Over the course of only one day, it became this big thing, which is the opposite of what I wanted. I wanted the situation to disappear. I understood that the more people knew, the bigger and more complicated it would get. Even worse, the more likely it would be that I would have to tell the real truth about what had happened to me when I was 12.

"It's not true," I finally admitted. "He didn't make me. I agreed to have sex with him. I was drunk, but it wasn't forced."

They were so confused and, understandably, concerned.

"Why would you make something like that up?" Craig's mother asked.

"I was just ashamed," I told her, probably the truest thing I had ever said.

By the time I told Craig, things were already over between us. Now, I was a cheater *and* a liar. And not just a normal liar. I used rape to try to hide an indiscretion.

Craig was so sweet. He didn't even know how to be angry with me. He was just confused. And he wasn't alone.

"What do you mean he didn't rape you?" Teresa asked when I told her.

"I don't know," I tried to explain. "You asked me, and you seemed so convinced that I just felt like it was easier to say yes."

"Easier?" she balked. "Are you blaming me for this?"

"No," I tried to backtrack, but it was too late. My freshman year wasn't even over, and in 24 hours, I had just burned a number of bridges. She wanted nothing to do with me after that, understandably so. Since Teresa and I still hung out with most of our high school friends, it became clear that I needed to find a new group.

I knew just who I should start hanging out with.

The kids from my school went out and had fun, but there was another group who had a lot more fun. When my friends went home from the bar at midnight, these kids stayed up partying into the morning. A lot of them already used coke and did drugs I hadn't even heard of yet. By now, I had learned how to be a chameleon, quickly switching my colors to fall into the new crowd.

Part of that crowd was a guy I had seen around campus for some time. Brian was attractive, funny, and a total player. He liked to party hard, and I never saw him with the same girl twice.

Now that we were part of the same group, we started going home together.

The thing was, once the sun rose, Brian wanted nothing to do with me. I can see now we were both using each other. At the time, however, I was the one feeling used.

I kept thinking more would come of it, that somehow Brian would wake up one day and realize I was the catch he'd been waiting for. But most mornings, he just seemed irritated that I was there, until we found each other at the bar again and repeated the same toxic cycle.

Before the days of cell phones and texting, Facebook stalking and Insta-tracking people, unhealthy relationships relied only on a common love of drinking in dive bars and hooking up at 2 a.m. Sometimes I wouldn't run into him. Sometimes I would watch as he took home other girls.

My school work wasn't doing much better. I mean, I always knew how to get away with it. I knew how to do just enough to get a B so that my parents didn't get worried. But I wasn't into it the way I had been at the beginning. I was back to dialing it in, bored by class, and just waiting for the night to come so I could go out again and get drunk and, hopefully, see Brian.

I was obsessed. In a way, Brian was like a human version of an eating disorder. I would binge him and feel an escape. Then, the next day, I would purge, feeling power and control. After the fact, these encounters made me feel horrible about myself, yet there was something comfortable in that, like I deserved to feel horrible about myself.

Instead, I survived on shots of hard liquor and a stream of white lies I would tell teachers and friends and family about why I was missing class and my grades were dropping.

I don't know that I could even say I had friends. All I really had was people I partied with. Once again, I had isolated myself from people who actually cared about me and was, instead, all alone.

Just like in high school, I began to spiral.

It was almost like the chaos was a distraction for me. I was spending a ton of money on clothes and booze and this crazy, lavish lifestyle that I felt I needed to keep up. In college in Montana, of all places. I even tried cocaine a few times though I couldn't afford it, which was likely a saving grace.

My parents weren't going to bankroll my lifestyle, so I just kept adding more to my schedule. I started as a tutor then got jobs working as a receptionist at a hotel and then as a receptionist at a massage place. I was working so hard and so often, I barely made it to class, let alone kept my grades up.

Finally, I got a job working at a clothing store. I had moved off campus into my own apartment and, thus, needed even more money. I knew the store counted the money in the register, but I had gotten desperate. How was I going to pay rent? How was I going to pay for drinks?

Brian and I were still hooking up. I liked to call it friends with benefits, though we were neither friends nor were there any benefits beyond drunken sex. It was rare for him to even buy me a drink. More often than not, in fact, he put his drinks on my tab.

So, one day, when I was working late at the store, without even thinking about it, I pulled a $20 out of the till. I figured they would never miss it. The next day, I pulled out $40.

Much of the time, I would be alone in the store. When my friends came in, they would shoplift, and I would look the other way. They would take the clothes from the racks, and I would take the cash from the register. But who are we kidding? I was stealing clothes too.

The sickest part was that I was smart enough to know I was going to get caught.

There were cameras in the store, and it was just a matter of time before someone at corporate saw what was going on or someone in accounting realized that the shortchange on the register wasn't an error.

It was like I had no moral compass. I would unleash my friends on the store with the warning, "Just don't get caught."

I was back to being someone I didn't recognize, and I didn't care. That might have been the most heartbreaking part. It wasn't just that I had become so removed from that sweet girl who loved music; it was that I didn't even mourn her anymore.

I might have been cold in high school; in college, I was becoming hard.

Eventually, my day came. I will never forget the morning I walked into work and noticed someone behind the register I had never seen before.

He introduced himself as a regional manager from the store. He smiled gently before asking, "Hey, Emily, can we have a word with you?"

I felt my stomach plunge to the floor. That moral compass that had felt so absent suddenly came back online.

I knew I had done something wrong; I just thought there was a way I wouldn't have to pay the price.

Chapter Five:
First Consequences

"We know you've been stealing, Emily," the manager said as he sat across from me in the back office. He was actually an investigator with the company, and they had been watching me for some time.

I tried my best to get out of it. Even though there was a lot about my lifestyle that was wild, I still looked relatively innocent. My hair was long and curled. I was wearing a knee-length dress and had a sweet, innocent face. I was just a college coed studying hard and working at a clothing store to pay for her rent.

"I don't know what you're talking about," I lied. I wish I could say it was hard for me to do, but I had been lying all my life. Now, it just really mattered.

The investigator just shook his head. He even looked like he felt a little sorry for me as he announced, "We have it all on tape. The cameras, Emily."

Over the next couple of hours, I tried to charm my way out of the crimes he now detailed to me: my own personal theft of merchandise and money and my friends' theft.

I tried everything I could, ultimately trying to offer him a sob story about how I didn't have any money and this was the only way I could survive, but I am sure what he saw on those tapes was a girl who could care less.

And his version was the honest one.

Until I was faced with consequences, I didn't care. I just moved through, making mistakes and burning bridges.

"Can I call my parents?" I finally asked.

"I'm afraid not," he told me, just as there was a knock at the door.

Two cops entered the room as the investigator stood up.

"I'm sorry," were his last words to me as the police began to read me my rights, sliding the handcuffs around my wrists and leading me out of the store, in front of customers and my colleagues.

I don't know how, but I still couldn't understand the gravity of what was happening. Maybe it was just that I was back in that moment of trauma; my brain was checking out, leaving me unable to comprehend my reality.

As the cops led me to the police car, I actually asked one of them, "Do I have to sit in the back?"

He looked at me as though I'd lost my mind, and, in a lot of ways, I had.

"Hon, you've just been arrested. Do you understand you're in big trouble?"

It was my turn to look at him like his head was missing.

I figured I would lose my job and have to pay back the money, but I didn't think it would go beyond that.

Even as I was driven to the police station and booked, I believed they would let me go, and it would be over. They took my prints and a mug shot. I went to sit in the cell until they told me that I could call a bail bondsman and get released.

By that point, I was too embarrassed to call my parents. Instead, I posted my own bail and went home to my apartment.

I told my roommates about it but still was not grasping the gravity of what happened. I mean, I knew I had done wrong, but I still didn't get it. I was so caught up in my own lies, I was absolutely removed from the reality of my situation. I let a week go by and pretended nothing happened. I didn't answer my phone. I didn't call anyone. I didn't take any action. I just waited though I didn't know what I was waiting for.

One of my roommates asked me, "When do you go to court? What does your lawyer say?"

Her questions slapped me back to reality. I realized I was going to have to face the next step. I had to do something. Finally, I called my parents.

It was the worst phone call I've ever made.

"Mom, I was fired," I began before telling her the hard part. "I was fired for stealing money."

Shock, horror, tears, questions...I don't even remember what she said. Then my dad got on the phone.

"Okay," he said, trying to stay calm. "We better get you a lawyer."

That's when it finally hit me. It finally got through. I was in really big trouble.

I had gotten so good at getting away with it, I figured it would be no different this time. The sad truth is that if I hadn't been a pretty, young white girl, my consequences would have been much worse. There is a really good chance that I would have never had the opportunities that led me to where I am today.

I might have ended up serving real time. I might have gotten caught up in the system.

My life could have gone in a million and one different directions.

Despite the severity of the charges—the money and merchandise totaled the exact amount to register as felony theft in the state of Montana—my parents hired an amazing lawyer. When the lawyer told my family and I what we were up against, that I could face real prison time for my actions, I saw my father cry for the first time. As a parent now, I can only imagine the pain they felt.

Word began to get out about what I did, and, in addition to being the topic of hot gossip, more people started to distance themselves from me. I lost more friends, causing me to lower my standards for friendship yet again. I started hanging out with people who drank and partied even harder. My life just kept getting darker and darker.

Here I had been stealing to keep up appearances, to make myself look better and richer than I was; in the end, all I had done was give people one more thing to whisper about behind my back.

I had also caused damage to my family. Clearly there was something wrong with me, but they didn't know what to do.

My dad always said, "You can be your own best friend or your own worst enemy."

His words were never truer. But how do you befriend someone you hate?

A few months into my case, my mom and I were walking around the mall together, the one place where we were able to talk. For some reason, conversation always flowed around the food court.

"Why did you do this?" she asked as we passed the Mrs. Field's Cookies. "What were you thinking at the time?"

My sweet mom. I loved her on a level she could never understand, but I also never felt that I could let her fully see who I was. Maybe because I did love her so much. I just wanted to protect her.

I didn't believe she could handle knowing who I was. I knew that, no matter what, she would find a way to blame herself for my mistakes.

"I just got desperate. I lost my way, I guess," I told her as though I was talking about the past when things were far from better.

She didn't know about the drugs, the sex, the eating issues. Instead, I just made it about money. I dumbed down the story like always to make it easier for other people to digest.

"I guess I didn't realize what I was doing was actually that bad," I explained, the lies just too easy to tell. "I worked so hard; I didn't think they would notice."

Though all those things were technically true, I couldn't tell her the real truth. I didn't care what happened to me because I didn't care about myself.

All I could do to make myself feel better was binge, purge, party, have sex, and drink. That same summer, a girl I grew up with died from her eating disorder. She was one of the few people who knew about mine. Maybe because of that, maybe because I was just too overwhelmed and shut down—combined with the fact that I wasn't allowed to leave the city limits because of my criminal charges—I didn't make it to her funeral. It took me many years to heal from the guilt of that.

Instead, I started drinking even more. I had to return to school that fall because I had no other choice, but people I had been friends with now outwardly ignored me. Even if people didn't know what happened or simply didn't care, I felt self-conscious and guilty and embarrassed everywhere I went. I wanted to isolate and escape. I started drinking before class to take the edge off the anxiety.

One of the people who continued to pay attention to me was Brian. Of course, that was only for a few hours after the bar. Brian lived with a few other roommates, plus, there were always random friends crashing on couches and coming in at all hours of the night. After waking up there more than a few times, I got to know many of them pretty well.

One night, I went home from the bar with one of Brian's roommates instead. Travis and I dated briefly. I wasn't that into him, but I hoped that by dating him, I might make Brian jealous.

It worked temporarily—enough that I wound up back in his bed. I wasn't the first girl to bounce between the two roommates.

My relationship with Brian had become a sick game of cat and mouse, only I'm not sure who was the cat and who was the mouse. At one low point, I even slept with both of them on the same night, partially out of desperation, partially out of revenge.

The year continued on, and I hopped from court appointments to the bar to class to work to Brian's apartment where I was now sleeping with Travis. Finally, I was sentenced to community service, with a deferred sentence that would be expunged from my record in a year, all in great part due to my lawyer.

Again, there could have been a million and one different outcomes, but I experienced the luckiest of them all.

When it was over, my lawyer stopped me as we began to walk out of the courtroom after thanking him.

"I just want to know, Emily. Why did you do it? I'm not going to tell your parents. It's just between us. But why did you really do it?"

I could have told him all the reasons I had offered my parents. I could have given one of my bullshit excuses. But I didn't. I told him the truth. "I don't know," I said. "I really don't know."

For the rest of the year, I threw myself into school, community service, and work, determined to be done with the charges and pay my restitution. I wanted to move on with my life. I was living in the same college town, I was still drinking, but now I had the added accessory of my very own probation officer. I was 18.

I couldn't take a legal drink but had already consumed a lifetime worth of booze and had been charged with a felony crime.

I was still hooking up with Travis, but, as usual, I was getting bored. One night, after he passed out, I decided I wanted to go home. Since this was in the era of landlines and answering machines, I tiptoed into the dark living room to call a friend to see if she could pick me up. Before I could dial, Brian's friend, Wes, awkwardly woke up on the couch I just sat down on.

Wes had always creeped me out. He was quiet and gave me weird looks. Then again, he had been watching me hop between Travis and Brian's bedrooms, so I just chalked it up to that.

But now Wes was on the couch next to me.

"So, I guess it's my turn, huh?" he commented as he tried to put his arm around me.

"I don't think so," I responded with a giggle, trying to keep it friendly.

But Wes kept pushing, telling me that he was next, and trying to kiss me. I said no again, but it quickly got to the point where it wasn't funny or friendly anymore. There was no question that I wasn't interested, yet he insisted.

I knew I could call for Travis. I could call for Brian. I could scream, "Rape!" But who would even believe me? Why *wouldn't* I just move onto another guy?

I kept saying no, but it didn't matter.

I just lay there on the couch, frozen. It was a very familiar feeling. Afterwards, I broke down. I couldn't stop crying. I walked a very long way home. I walked past a hospital and considered going to the ER and asking for a rape kit. But I knew I couldn't tell anyone what had actually happened. I had already used my card. I truly believed that no one would believe me. I told my roommate that Wes hit on me to explain why I was so upset. After all, she thought he was creepy too. But that was it. Now I had yet another secret to keep.

In a way, it was one I felt I deserved. I was now a cheater, a bitch, a slut, a liar, and a thief. I was asking for whatever terrible thing happened to me.

The one thing I did know without a doubt was that I was done with Montana. I never again went over to Brian's. In fact, I never spoke to any of them again. I told my parents I needed a fresh start. I had no more bridges left to burn.

I wanted out of Montana. I wanted to go somewhere warm and sunny. I applied to a school in Southern California and was accepted.

I was ready for another do-over, but, as they say, wherever you go, there you are.

Chapter Six:
Identity Crisis

The first thing I did after arriving in Los Angeles, having been accepted by one of its top schools, was dye my hair California blonde. Unlike back in Montana, no one knew me on the west coast. I didn't have any baggage or history. No one was whispering about me in the halls. I was just Emily from Montana, a cute (and now blonde!) good girl going to a good school.

I knew this was my big chance to start over, as though a new space and a new place might suddenly turn me into someone different.

Later, I would find out that people call this "pulling a geographic."

Many of us believe that by going to a new town, starting a new school, entering a new marriage, beginning a new *anything*, we'll be different people. Because our new friends won't know about our past, they won't be able to judge us.

Dying my hair was only part of pulling a geographic. I believed if I looked like a different person, I might become one, and, in turn, I might be able to avoid my old behaviors.

Alas, science has shown that when people adapt to different environments, their personalities can take on characteristics of the new place, but their core personalities—their strengths and defects—remain relatively unchanged.

I arrived on campus ready to become the better version of myself, and, at first, the blonde hair and the missing baggage seemed to work.

I made friends, I joined a sorority, and then I met a guy.

"What's your name?" Julian asked, leaning against the wall at my new sorority house.

Julian was a senior, and we had never met anyone like each other before. He was from Newport Beach and though I didn't know it at the time, he was the kind of rich I had never encountered. Sure, I had friends with money in Montana, but Julian had access to his own helicopter.

To him, I was exotic simply because I was from Montana and still had my original boobs. He had never hooked up with a girl with real boobs before, which is kind of scary when you think about it.

He was everything to me. Rich, handsome, sophisticated.

He was out of the movie I thought my life in California would be.

I had moved in with a roommate, joined a sorority, and, now, within just a few weeks, I was dating one of the most eligible seniors on campus.

I had only been there a month, and the move was already a complete success.

"Do you want to go shopping?" Julian asked one afternoon after he picked me up at my apartment.

"Of course," I replied innocently, clicking in the seatbelt of his convertible BMW. I imagined we would go shopping like I did with my mom in Montana: window shopping, chatting, and stopping by the food court for lunch.

His version was a little different.

Julian pulled up at the South Coast Plaza where I quickly found out we were going on a *Pretty Woman*-style shopping spree. I had one credit card I had signed up for when I arrived on campus, having been offered immediate approval by one those kiosks they have at orientation. I received a free t-shirt and a high-interest credit card emblazoned with the school logo.

I pulled it out at South Coast Plaza, not wanting to look like I couldn't fit in.

By the second week of dating Julian, I was already in debt.

I had become this other girl—blonde, sexy, and with money to burn—yet none of it was true. Once again, I was lying. Except now I didn't have to say a word to do it.

When I arrived in Los Angeles, I promised myself I wouldn't drink. After what had happened with Wes, I knew alcohol just brought on terrible things. I was exhausted by its consequences and decided that if I could just stay away from booze, I would be able to handle everything else—the new school, the new boyfriend, the new me. I promised myself I'd be honest. I told Julian my hair wasn't really blonde.

That was a good start for me. But the honesty didn't last long, at least not once I started drinking again.

As Annie Grace writes in *This Naked Mind*, "We've been conditioned to believe we enjoy drinking. We think it enhances our social life and relieves boredom and stress. We believe these things below our conscious awareness. This is why, even after we consciously acknowledge that alcohol takes more than it gives, we retain the desire to drink."

By week three, that desire had returned.

Julian and I would go out, and since he was 21, he would order cocktails or a bottle of wine. After a few dates, I felt strange saying I didn't want anything. We were in college. Everyone drank. I didn't want to be the weird new girl who failed to have a beer in her hand at the party.

Joining a sorority didn't help either.

Greek life pretty much demanded that you binge. Though I had made it nearly two months without alcohol, it was hard to say no when Julian offered me a glass of champagne on our third date.

The minute it went down my throat, I relaxed. Once again, I felt that great escape: freedom from anxiety.

I didn't realize how anxious I had been since arriving in California.

Once I started drinking, I forgot about everything that had happened in Montana. I didn't worry about pretending to be someone else. The booze allowed me to be whoever I wanted to be. It made the lie real.

I always made friends easily, and California was no different.

Between the sorority and my heavy class load, I felt like I was back on the inside. I wasn't hanging out with shady characters or people who regularly stole clothing from stores. I felt normal.

Julian only added to that. We went to fancy restaurants and parties, and he bought me nice things. Of course, that credit card came in handy, as I bought dresses and makeup and handbags and shoes to match the life I was suddenly living.

Though I drank, I didn't look any different from Julian or my friends at school.

My geographic had apparently fixed that too.

Sometimes I might have drunk a little too much, but so did most of the girls in my sorority. I was able to dedicate myself to school once again, attending all my science classes, participating in study groups, and spending late nights at the library.

One afternoon, I was sitting around with a group of my sorority sisters at a tailgate on campus when we started talking about birth control.

"I'm not even on the pill," I confessed.

One of them laughed. "What? You didn't think you'd be having sex out here?"

"Girl, you better get on something," another added. "Not that Julian can't afford to take care of it if you get pregnant…if you know what I mean."

Dating someone everyone knew was rich always brought on comments like that. People would look at me differently, and I definitely saw how Julian's wealth brought him immediate access wherever he went, whether it was a dumb frat party on campus or the Sky Bar on the Sunset Strip.

All he had to do was walk up to the door, say his name, and people let him in. He had the kind of confidence only money could buy, which only made me feel more insecure. He was actually a sweet, kind boyfriend, but I wasn't kind to myself.

I still had so much self-hatred for what had happened, so much shame, some of which I had earned, some which had been placed upon me.

When I was with Julian, it felt like the seas parted for us, but it wasn't until I had a few drinks that I could wade through them with confidence.

To make it easier on myself, I started pre-partying so that I didn't have to feel insecure until I had that first cocktail at the party. At first, it was just a drink or two before Julian picked me up, but then the hangover would be so bad from the previous night, it was easier to chase it with a drink and keep it going until the evening arrived.

There were still a lot of days in which I would make it to class and be sober and alert, back to raising my hand and participating, but there were even more days in which I would barely make it to class, too sick to show up at Monday night dinner at the sorority house, or feigning sickness so I could stay in bed while Julian went out to enjoy the day.

Finally, I listened to my sorority sisters and went to the university clinic to get on the pill.

The minute the doctor walked into the room, I felt weird.

According to the National Center for Victims of Crime, children who have experienced rape or attempted rape in their adolescent years are 13.7 times more likely to experience rape or attempted rape in college. Sadly, those with a prior history of sexual victimization are also extremely likely to be re-victimized, with some research estimating an increased risk of over 1000 percent.

I don't know if knowing that might have changed anything for me that day. If the weird feeling I'd had about the doctor might have propelled me from the room. I had already been raped once in college. How many times did I really have to be assaulted?

The worst part was, unlike with Evan and Wes, I didn't even realize that was what happened to me that day.

All I knew was that the doctor seemed terribly inappropriate. He didn't use gloves when he examined me, he didn't give me anything to cover myself with, and he touched me and talked to me in a way that was unnecessary for a physical exam. But I was only 19. Though I'd racked up sexual partners, I had probably only had two or three gynecological exams in my life, and they were with our family doctor in my hometown, the same man who delivered me when I was a baby. I didn't have a good comparison.

I had no idea what was happening was illegal. I had no idea it was assault. All I knew was that I felt weird when I slipped off the table and back into my clothes.

Did something bad just happen? I asked myself. *And, if it didn't, why did I suddenly feel so horrible?*

It would take many years and a major lawsuit to learn what really happened to me that day, along with hundreds of other students over the course of three decades at the same school. I had been victimized yet again, and though I didn't consciously understand it at the time, I responded just as I did to every confusing thing in my life.

I began to drink more.

And with the drinking, my lies only continued to increase. It was just like when I was a kid, saying I had a horse and six cats, but, now, people paid more attention.

I don't know how Julian didn't see the lies, but I think that was the blessing of dating a young, debonair rich guy. He was too into himself to pay much attention to what I said and did. If he had been watching, he would surely have seen that his girlfriend was spiraling.

The nights would start out nice enough. We would go to a party and have a few drinks, but now there was cocaine and other drugs too.

By the end of the night, I would be one of the last ones awake, somehow hanging out with a different crowd than at the start of the night. I wouldn't even know what I had said. Every morning I became a detective of my night before.

I couldn't keep anything straight. I might have made up a new personality since moving to California, but, now, I had no idea who I was.

Chapter Seven:
A New Bottom

It's funny how the body will do for us what we cannot do for ourselves. I was on a crash course to oblivion, desperately spending money to keep up with Julian and drinking till I blacked out. Between my hangovers and drunken nights, I was still caught up in my eating disorder.

Controlling food had become second nature. Sometimes I would be able to stay away from the bathroom, getting a handle on that frantic urge, but as soon as the rest of my life started spinning out of control, I would fall back into the binge-and-purge habit. I was desperate for the freedom eating gave me and the freedom that came when I got rid of it.

When I couldn't predict the outcome of anything else in my life, I could at least tell what was going to happen when I leaned over the toilet bowl and excised everything inside me.

I would watch that number on the scale decline and know that though I was powerless over Julian, my drinking, and everything else in life, I held power over those digits.

Then I got sick.

It started with my hair. Whenever I would take a shower, large chunks of my long blonde hair would come out in my hand. Then my heart started racing and beating irregularly. I was feverish and nauseated all the time. I didn't know what it was, but I knew something was wrong. Finally, I went to the doctor, fearing that my behavior had finally caught up with me.

The results came back. I was suffering from Graves' disease.

Graves' disease is an autoimmune disorder that causes hyperthyroidism, or overactive thyroid. Basically, your immune system attacks the thyroid and causes it to make more thyroid hormone than your body needs. The thyroid is a small, butterfly-shaped gland in the front of your neck that controls how your body uses energy. It affects nearly every organ in your body—even the way your heart beats.

As I later found out, there is a direct connection between thyroid functioning and alcohol use, as alcohol can depress the thyroid gland and cause physical imbalance and strain.

Acetaldehyde, the compound that causes hangovers, will frequently interfere with thyroid hormone receptors, triggering the thyroid gland to become overworked. Too much acetaldehyde can also cause symptoms of hypothyroidism, even when the thyroid is functioning normally.

I was suffering from a thyroid condition and fueling it with alcohol.

The good thing about Graves' is that it's fairly easy to treat. I was given a prescription for a daily medication that, when taken properly, reduces or eliminates most of the side effects of the disease.

The only problem, as I quickly found out, was that the medication made me gain weight. My weight was the only thing I could control, and now that was being taken from me.

As much as I knew that I needed to take the medication, and sometimes would, I started playing around with it, trying to avoid it when I had an event or a big party.

The party was the only thing that mattered to me.

Once again, I had abandoned school for alcohol. I was barely making it to class, and, most nights, when I went out and got drunk, I couldn't even remember what happened.

As Sarah Hepola writes in *Blackout*, "I wanted the gift of forgetting. The blackouts were horrible. It was hideous to let those nights slide into a crack in the ground. But even scarier was to take responsibility for the mess I'd made. Even scarier was to remember your own life."

Studies have shown that though alcohol is necessary for a blackout, it has less to do with the amount consumed and more with the circumstances around its consumption. Some people don't blackout when they're drinking more than usual. More frequently, blackouts are connected with how much food you have in your stomach, whether you're a woman or a man, and the way in which the alcohol gets consumed.

Blackouts were really just a matter of timing, and I was *always* on time.

Women are at a much higher risk of blackouts because we have significantly less water in our system, which means the alcohol is less diluted. Additionally, we have a significantly lower concentration of the enzyme that metabolizes alcohol before it passes into the bloodstream. We also have more body fat, which makes it more difficult for our bodies to absorb alcohol.

Since drinking on an empty stomach increases the risk of blacking out, I frequently found myself losing parts of the night, if not the whole night. Though sometimes I would be able to remember fragments, there were so many mornings when the last few hours before I passed out had vanished.

As I later found out, I was experiencing what they call en bloc blackouts, which happens when information is not successfully transferred from short-term to long-term memory, kind of like trauma. I might have been there in the moment, but all memory would soon be erased.

My life was existing only in the short-term. I didn't have any long-term goals or hopes. I just wanted to make it to the next weekend, the next party, the next drink, the next purge. I couldn't think about tomorrow, and last night was usually gone. I was trapped in a terrible present, but I didn't know how to get out.

Instead, I just put on a cute outfit, cut my remaining hair shorter, tried to cover my blotchy skin with makeup, and avoided looking into my own eyes in the mirror before I walked into the bar, the restaurant, or the party and pretended everything was fine.

It was all just another lie, and people were beginning to see through it.

My sorority sisters started asking me if I was okay, but, now, I had an answer. Graves' disease gave me a way out of other people's concerns.

Even Julian was beginning to ask if I was okay.

"Yeah. It's just this thyroid thing," I told him as we drove to meet his family in Orange County.

"Are you sure?" he looked at me briefly. "You have heartburn all the time now, and, well, it seems like you've been drinking a lot. I mean, please don't get mad, but you just look tired. And you've put on weight."

Thanks, Romeo, I thought though I knew he was right.

Julian graduated from college that spring and started working in Beverly Hills. We were beginning to see a lot less of each other. Maybe that's why he was worried.

It's easier to ignore someone is fading when you see them every day, but when it's been a couple of weeks, the disappearing act becomes visible.

And I was disappearing.

I didn't feel comfortable at my sorority house where the other girls' concerns began to feel like prying.

The last time Julian dropped me off at my apartment, he looked at me sadly and said, "Just take care of yourself, Emily. You're a really special girl."

I saw in his eyes the reflection I kept avoiding in the mirror, but I also saw something else. I was damaged.

As he drove away that day, I knew he wouldn't be coming back.

I decided that what I needed to do was throw myself back into my classes. Thankfully, there was someone at school who made that incredibly easy.

Jake was a graduate assistant in one of my classes. He was older and handsome and smart, and, unlike Julian, he really liked to party. He made no secret of his interest in me, so once Julian had one foot out the door, I fixed my attention on Jake.

As an added bonus, he hung out with people outside of our school. Another network for me to blend into and, thus, avoid my sorority sisters.

There was a popular restaurant his friend owned where everyone would gather to party after the restaurant closed. They all did lots of drugs; since I liked to fit in, I started participating.

Now, in addition to battling Graves' disease, failing to take my medication, drinking to blackout, and either binging and purging or avoiding eating altogether, I was adding cocaine and other drugs to the mix.

As one can imagine, I looked amazing.

Still, the more attention I paid Jake, the more attention he paid me.

We started hooking up. Even though I knew we weren't supposed to be seeing each other (he was my teacher in a way), I felt drawn to him. The fact that I wasn't supposed to be seeing him made it that much more intoxicating. I was looking for escape however I could get it.

I just needed someone so I didn't feel alone. I needed someone who could make me feel like what I was doing was okay.

I've heard it called "lower companions," but I can't say I was much better. Though some of Jake's friends were doing heroin, and I drew the line at shooting up, I was right alongside them as we did drugs all night at the restaurant, emerging into the early morning light like vampires with big sunglasses.

It had only been a couple of months when Jake invited me to a party.

"Make sure you dress up. Something sexy," he told me before letting me know a limo would be coming to get me. That wasn't really Jake's style, so I should have known something was strange, but I was long past the place where I could see red flags. My whole life was a red flag.

Instead I got in the back of the empty limo as it drove us across town to a big mansion in the Holly-wood Hills. As soon as I walked through the door, I wondered if I could catch the limo home.

It was like something out of *Eyes Wide Shut*. It was like a kinky horror show. Some people were fully clothed, some were stark naked, and there was everything and anything in between.

I might have been dabbling in the darker side of life, but I was still a modest girl from Montana in so many ways. I had never seen anything like this. This was before porn on the internet, and it was absolutely shocking.

"Emily," Jake said, coming up behind me, kissing my neck, and putting his arm around my waist.

"Jake, what the hell is this?"

"Crazy, huh?" He smiled devilishly, as though he was just as shocked by it as I was. Then he grabbed my hand and led me upstairs to a private bedroom. I was confused why he would have brought me all the way here just to have sex. We could have done that anywhere.

He gave me a glass of champagne though I had been drinking long before the limo arrived and during the entire ride.

We walked into the room where another woman waited. A brunette woman, pretty, older, probably Jake's age. He didn't introduce us as he brought me to the bed.

"Jake, what's going on?" I asked, but he was already in the process of taking off my dress and pushing me down on the bed.

I had no clue what was happening, but I didn't even know how to say no anymore. I was so exhausted, so used to checking out when this happened.

I lay there, drunk, and let Jake have sex with me, all while this woman watched from the corner.

When he was done, he leaned over and looked at the woman.

"Well?" he asked her.

She shrugged. "I think you can do better."

Still naked underneath Jake, I looked back and forth between him and the woman.

Finally, I got my voice back. "Wait, what?" I said. "Who are you?"

The woman barely smiled. "I'm his wife."

What? WHAT?

I was shocked.

I felt like I should apologize though I don't know why. Clearly, she was fine with what just happened. I never thought to ask if he was married. At the age of 20, it wasn't a question I was accustomed to asking new boyfriends.

"We've been looking for someone to join us," Jake explained, but I still didn't understand. "To live with us," Jake continued. "Serve us."

It began to dawn on me, Jake and his wife were looking for a sex servant, and I had just been interviewed.

His wife stood up. "See you downstairs," she said.

Apparently, I had just failed the interview though I can say with certainty that I would not have been interested in the position.

I pushed Jake off me and got dressed while he stammered and apologized and tried to explain himself out of an unexplainable situation. After pleading with him to just let me go home, he finally called a taxi, and I went back downstairs alone, rushing past the throng of naked bodies and sex toys and bondage and things that had never been part of my vocabulary.

I got into the cab and broke down in tears.

For the previous few months, Jake had become the center of my life. I had distanced myself from most of my friends at school by now. The only people I hung out with were Jake's friends; now, they were all gone too.

I vowed to avoid Jake, which meant avoiding class. My time at school was already splintering, but now I didn't want to go to class at all.

All I wanted to do was drink.

I was falling apart again, and I wasn't sure how to stop it. I wasn't sure I wanted to.

Chapter Eight:
Intervention #1

"Emmy," my mother offered over the phone. "I think it's time for you to come home."

I stood at a pay phone in a Los Angeles psychiatric hospital knowing she was right, though my home had now changed.

During my first year in California, my parents had bought a house in southern Oregon, leaving Montana after nearly 20 years.

They asked me to move back in with them so I could get better. I still wasn't sure what "getting better" meant.

I had only been in the psychiatric hospital for a few days, but it was clear something was broken. It was ultimately my sorority sisters who made the call.

Over the previous couple of months, they had grown concerned. I knew that Graves' disease wasn't enough to keep them off my back, so I concocted another story.

"I have cancer," I told Hannah, one of the first girls I had become friends with at the sorority. "It's why I haven't been around. It's why I've been so sick."

Hannah nearly burst into tears upon hearing the news, and, at that point, I wished I did have cancer. I was so horrified by my life, I wanted to die.

Then the lie began to unravel. I thought that I was exhibiting all the symptoms: I was throwing up all the time, my hair was falling out, I could barely attend class. But I also had a lot of other symptoms: coming home wasted, blacking out at parties, and generally falling apart in public.

They knew something was wrong, and when they finally confronted me, I had to admit that it wasn't cancer. *I* was the cancer.

At that point, I didn't have a lot of friends. Not real friends, and certainly none who knew the real me. Most of the people I hung out with were men, and they were far from real friends, just guys I partied with. I was absolutely cut off from anyone who loved or cared about me, including myself.

I had become my own worst enemy.

Thankfully, those girls at the sorority house cared more about me than I did. They called my parents and then drove me to the psychiatric hospital.

As we drove along the 10 freeway in Los Angeles, I didn't have any fight left. It was a rare rainy day in LA, but I was an emotional desert, unable to connect with any joy or pain.

I couldn't even cry as my friends left. I just watched the door close behind them.

When I was processed for intake, I didn't know how to tell the truth. I knew I had a problem with food, but I couldn't see what the alcohol was doing. I didn't even have the words to describe my relationship with booze.

The problem with alcohol is that everyone does it. In fact, as I got older and continued to drink (spoiler alert!), I discovered that it was easy to hide my drinking problem because other people drank with similar abandon. In college, my problem was especially easy to disguise.

Though my consequences looked more severe, my behaviors weren't that different from everyone else's.

But I knew the bulimia was wrong. Though bulimia affects 4.7 million females and 1.5 million males, I admitted to binging and purging during my intake meeting, leading doctors to believe that I was only dealing with an eating disorder. One diagnosis was enough for me.

They asked what medication I took, and I had trouble answering the question. I didn't want to tell them about the thyroid medication because then they would make me take it.

I was in a psychiatric hospital, yet I was worried that if they gave me too high a dosage of thyroid medication, I would gain weight.

"Have you ever experienced a sexual assault?"

The doctor was gentle as he asked the question. Maybe he could see it written across my face. Maybe he could see it in my frail shoulders, which looked like they might break from an invisible weight. Maybe he could see it in my thinning hair, which I couldn't cover up in there. Maybe he could see it in my swollen, bloodshot eyes, which I quickly averted when he asked the question.

I told him the same story I had been offering people since I slept with my first boyfriend, Mike. It was a boy at another school. I didn't say no, but I didn't say yes.

Then I stopped myself.

"It was a boy at camp," I shared, getting myself one step closer to the truth, but not all the way. I couldn't say the boy was a man. I couldn't explain what happened. At that point, I still couldn't remember much from that afternoon. "And something happened at my last school," I added, tears welling up in my eyes. I wanted to tell. I wanted to feel the rain. I wanted to burst into tears and tell him about Evan and Wes and Jake.

But when the therapist asked if I wanted to talk about it, I shook my head no.

I had gone far enough. I was afraid if I said too much, they might ring a bell. My parents would be called; a big deal would be made.

If I didn't want to talk about it, I certainly didn't want anyone else participating in the conversation. It was like the bulimia: if I offered them just enough of my truth, I could protect the parts I didn't want to discuss.

The therapist asked me why I threw up, and it didn't take me long to respond.

"I'm supposed to be perfect."

"No one is supposed to be perfect," he responded, shaking his head gently. "No one *is* perfect."

I shrugged my shoulders. "I used to be perfect."

I didn't actually believe that, but I did know that at one point, life seemed to come much easier, and now it all felt so hard.

"How do you feel when you throw up?"

I smiled, maybe for the first time since arriving at the hospital. "Relief," I said.

He asked if I drank a lot, and I shrugged. "No more than anyone else."

I could share about my eating disorder, but that was enough. Like my sexual past, subconsciously, I knew I had to protect the drinking because there are some things that, once said, can never be taken back.

Now I can see that even my partial truths were all baby steps towards healing. Like reconstructive surgery, I had to take it in parts, managing each piece as I went, moving forward when I could, sometimes falling behind.

They say the arc of history is long, but it always bends towards justice.

I like to think the arc of trauma is long too, but if we're lucky, it can bend towards healing. I was heading in the right direction, even if it would take me a lot more time, and a lot more mistakes, to get there.

I didn't know how to love myself during those days in the hospital, but I knew enough to understand that my mom was right when she said it was time to come home.

I stood in the hallway, staring at the chipped nail polish on my toes, wearing hospital-issued flip flops.

"Okay, Mom," I agreed. I felt like I was back at music camp.

I wanted to run in to her arms and cry. I wanted her to hold me and rub my back and make it all okay, but, once again, the words weren't there.

"You know," my mom struggled to say, "I saw you in the bathroom once, your feet going the wrong way. I didn't want to believe it was really true."

It was a relief and a slap in the face at the same time: A relief to know she didn't think I was perfect and was okay with it, and a slap in the face to think that she didn't do anything about it. But what could she have done? I would have lied it away.

And she probably knew that. She said it herself: she didn't want to believe it. Now she had to. We both had to.

The best I could do was agree to go home. It wasn't like I had many other choices.

There was no way I could go back to college in Southern California. I was embarrassed and ashamed and had once again burned so many bridges. Calling my sorority house to tell them I wouldn't be coming back was bad enough. I didn't want to step foot back on that campus—the place where I was assaulted by the gynecologist, was abused by a grad assistant, and had attempted to make a fresh start and ended up even more broken and traumatized than when I began.

Julian and my friend, Sasha, packed up two suitcases for me and picked me up from the hospital. It was a long quiet ride to the airport. I cried in the back seat under my sunglasses. I had hurt these two people so much, yet they were still showing me love. The problem was I couldn't accept it. I didn't understand why they were helping me; I wouldn't have.

"Get well, Emily. I mean that," Julian said, choking back tears. It was the last time I ever saw him.

I hugged Sasha for a long time. She promised to send the rest of my things and to call when I got home. I walked to the plane, crying.

I wish I could say I was sad or happy or hopeful as the plane took off, but the only thing I could feel was defeated.

I left LA on a typical sunny-and-hot California morning and landed in Oregon to a typical rainy-and-grey afternoon, an immediate contrast to the city I had been living in.

My parents picked me up from the airport, and I could tell by their voices that they were nervous. The minute they saw me, they knew something was wrong, more wrong than they initially were led to believe. I cried as soon as I got in the back seat of the car and most of the way home.

We had already been through the theft case, and, now, this. They might have been able to make excuses for what had happened at the store or why my feet were "going the wrong way" in the bathroom. Like a lot of parents, it was easier to live in denial than to face the fact that there was something wrong with their "perfect" daughter. But there was no space left for denial anymore.

This time, they threw themselves into getting me better. They found the name of a psychiatrist and a therapist who specialized in eating disorders and helped me find a local college where I could transfer credits. They watched me like ornithologists waiting for a baby bird to hatch, unsure if I would make it out of my shell.

But just like when I got busted for stealing, hitting bottom actually gave me the motivation to heal. The psychiatrist prescribed me a good combination of medications that immediately helped to relieve the depression and anxiety for the first time in my life. My hair, now back to its natural brown, began to grow back. My skin began to look better.

I quit drinking though I didn't draw much attention to it. It was as much a matter of circumstance as anything else.

I lived at home, had no friends, and never went out.

At dinner one night, my dad asked me, "Em, one thing we wonder, if you drank so much, how are you not an alcoholic?"

I didn't know the answer to that question. I wouldn't know for another 18 years. My father had just predicted the outcome. Instead of questioning my drinking, I focused on getting better, and once again, it looked like I was.

Chapter Nine:
A Fresh Start #3

I sat on another couch in another therapist's office though, this time, I was no longer in a hospital. I was at home living with my parents.

In LA, I just wanted to get out of the hospital. Now, I actually wanted to get better.

Though LA might have been the sunny town, I began to see the light in Oregon.

And the more I told the truth, the lighter I felt.

For the first time, I told my mom that I was raped. And I used the word rape. I didn't want my parents to feel guilty, so I still tried to make it sound like it wasn't premeditated, as though it had been a date rape between me and another classmate. I also didn't want them to feel guilty that I was raped at a camp they sent me to. As long as everyone thought it was another kid at school, I felt safe. I was able to keep my "I didn't say yes, but I didn't say no" story.

I didn't dare say it was a camp counselor. I worried that if I did, there would be legal repercussions. They could try to find Evan. I would have to tell the police.

I kept the whole truth to myself; I was used to the taste of my poison pill.

I could tell my mom almost felt relieved. It wasn't something they had done; it was something that had happened to me. And though a part of me felt more free, I was still processing a lie, a truth I tried to make myself believe.

I got what I wanted, but not what I needed.

Yet life got better.

Now that I wasn't drinking, and I was taking my medication as directed, my thyroid got better. My hair grew back, I was eating, and also working out. I felt healthy and strong. The darkness was once again fading, as was my own guilt.

I started taking classes again, and, just as I did in California and Montana before that, I felt good going back to school. It was the one place where my confidence hadn't been wrecked; it was the one thing I could rely on.

In fact, I became so focused, I didn't participate in anything social this time around. I didn't even realize my college had a football team until I was graduating. I made many friends in class and in lab but didn't socialize outside of school and was totally okay with that.

I just liked going to class and then coming home and doing my homework. I went to therapy in between.

My mom made dinner most nights, and I would sit with my parents and watch TV. I could tell they felt less nervous around me too. They were so happy to have me back and see that I was finally getting better. My mom and I went shopping together like we had when I was a teenager. I felt at home.

I began to get more honest with my psychiatrist, stayed on my medication, and, over time, the memories of California, Montana, and all the lies began to fade.

I applied for and got a job working in a hospital, still debating whether I would pursue a medical degree. Ironically, a dietician's office actually became a very healthy place for me. I would help create menus for patients based on their specific diet needs. I was familiar with counting calories and fat grams, and putting together healthy, balanced meal plans helped reinforce healthy habits of my own.

I was starting to make friends again at work. We would go out for drinks, but it didn't feel weird. I felt in control of it, able to have a beer or two and go home. Knowing that I was going home to my parents made it easier to reign it in.

I didn't leave with strangers or sleep with my friends' boyfriends.

I didn't snort coke at 2 a.m.

I was normal.

"You've come so far and accomplished so much," my therapist said during a session. "Do you feel like you finally got where you wanted to be?"

The first word that came to mind was, "No."

I knew there was so much more that hadn't been discussed, so many stories I failed to tell, but, on the outside, everything looked so good.

I smiled. "I think I finally made it through the darkness."

And it felt that way.

I didn't wake up wanting to die. I was grateful for my relationship with my parents. I thought everything was going really well.

Until it wasn't.

There was a guy at the hospital who was close to my age, and he asked me out for dinner.

I liked him enough, and it felt like it was time to begin casually dating again.

For over a year, I had remained single and celibate. My parent's house had become like my own little sober living house. Or, rather, a convent.

And now the nun was back out.

Jaxon and I would go and get dinner. Some nights I would stay at his place, but I didn't take it too seriously.

"I think we should get married," Jaxon shared as we sat across from one another at dinner. I didn't know what to say; I almost laughed.

We had only been dating a couple of months. I think he saw the look on my face and quickly backtracked. "I mean, not now," he said. "Just someday. I really like you, Emily."

It was one of those moments when you become so embarrassed for someone else, you know you can't recover. As nice as Jaxon was, I wasn't interested in marrying him.

He kept calling me, wanting to spend the weekend together, wanting to hang out every night after work.

Up until that point, I had been eating really well, but I didn't know how to handle the situation with

Jaxon. I once again felt like someone was forcing me into something.

I didn't say no, but I didn't say yes.

Instead, I ran away. I quit working at the hospital, got a job at a manufacturing company as a lab tech, and stopped returning Jaxon's calls. Eventually, he got the hint. I still had a hard time saying no.

By this point, I knew that you could lie through your words or you could lie through your actions.

Finally, Jaxon stopped calling, and I felt safe, but, by that point, I had begun to fall back into old habits, trying to regain control. I started working out too much and skipping meals. I began watching that number on the scale and responding to it. The number was in control of my mood that day and how I felt about myself.

I began to care again whether it ticked up or down. I got into working out, telling myself that as long as I wasn't purging, I wasn't engaging with the disorder. As long as I wasn't leaning over a toilet bowl, I was still healthy.

I really enjoyed my job and had finally established a good group of friends—mostly other college students like myself, normal people who weren't stealing from stores or going to sex parties.

It seemed like I was finally growing up.

Then I met Rich.

He had just started working as a manager in a different department at my company, but his reputation preceded him.

"My sister knows his ex-girlfriend, and she says she caught him cheating in their own bed," my co-worker Paula told me before we had even been on our first date.

I use the term "first date" loosely because Rich wasn't the type that went on first dates. He just took girls home from the bar and sometimes stuck around. But he was hot, and I was starting down that slippery slope of danger again.

I was immediately obsessed.

My friends were so confused. Again, they had gotten to know one version of Emily— responsible, smart, trustworthy—and then, suddenly, I was chasing after this loser.

"Oh my God, Em," Paula told me after Rich and I hooked up. "Don't bother. He is such a player!"

But the minute I heard someone was unavailable, I became determined to pin them down, no matter the consequences for myself.

I started going out more because Rich went out. We would get drunk and go back to his apartment and have sex.

He was nice enough to me, and I found him interesting and funny. But there was a dark side I couldn't figure out. He had boxes of unopened mail and receipts and seemed to have a lot of secrets. Obviously, I needed to fix him.

He would make comments about how he hated women but that I was cool.

"I don't get how men get so pussy whipped they even bother getting married," he would boast. "Not for me!"

I decided he just hadn't met the right woman yet, and I was definitely her.

I began to work out more, as always equating my size to my worth. I thought if only I was thinner, Rich would pay more attention to me, would desire me more. And as though that wasn't a slippery enough slope, I began to drink more and stay out later. I assumed if I wasn't the last woman left at the bar, he would probably take someone else home.

Rich became like my eating disorder, and the sicker I became, the more control I thought I had. Until I started losing all the control I had spent the previous year building.

By then, the lie had taken over.

Chapter Ten:
Old Habits Don't Die

When Ani DiFranco sang, "I am getting nowhere with you and I can't let you go, and I can't get through," she must have been dating Rich.

I couldn't get anywhere with him. I couldn't get through, yet I absolutely couldn't let go.

"What do you see in him anyway?" Paula asked me one day at lunch.

I looked out the window at the grey skies and tried to find the words to the feeling I felt so intensely when I was in his presence.

"It's like when we're alone, we're the only people in the world who matter."

"Yeah, but when he's not with you, it's like you barely matter at all," Paula replied with a know-it-all smirk.

I knew rumors had been circulating around work. It wasn't so different from high school or college. I came in all squeaky clean, but, through Rich, the other me had begun to resurface. Tales of me being shitfaced at the bar—and, even worse, tales of the things Rich did behind my back when we weren't at the bar—were whispered about in voices just loud enough to hear.

I would show up at work after a weekend and wonder what I had done and what my colleagues might have to say about it.

What made things worse was that I wasn't in high school anymore. I couldn't pretend that I was just like everyone else because, by now, it was becoming clear I wasn't.

I wasn't lying when I told Paula that it felt like Rich and I were the only two people in the world, but I think the feeling was even more pronounced by the fact that when we weren't alone, I barely existed to Rich.

Over the next few months, I would begin to wear him down. He told me he never wanted to get married and never wanted to have children, but being terrible with money and in debt, he also needed help paying rent. What a catch.

Since I was spending more and more time at his apartment, and he frequently borrowed my car while I was at work, it made sense that we split the rent and move in together.

I soon found out splitting the rent meant I paid for it and then gently tried to coax his half from him.

We both made close to the same amount, but while I was able to pay my bills and put some away, Rich's money burned a hole in his pocket.

Once again, I was isolating myself, choosing Rich over friends or my own health or happiness. Besides going to class, every other waking moment was spent seeking his attention. Then, when I got it, all I could do was worry about when it would go away.

By this point, my friends had once again begun to disappear. I was used to this process. I would make friends with nice, responsible girls, the kind who could have a couple of beers and go home early. Many of them were already getting engaged, some were getting married and preparing to have children.

At first, they thought I was one of them. I looked like them and acted like them, but then the old behaviors would emerge, and they wouldn't know who I was. They would back away until they were out of the friendship entirely.

"Don't you have any friends of your own?" Rich asked me as we drove to a birthday party for one of his buddies one evening.

Now that we were living together, I didn't have anywhere else to go. Rich's life was my life; his friends were my friends. I had my family, but they were no more fans of Rich than the people at work.

It was no surprise that my parents didn't like him. Rich didn't even get along with his own family.

I recently saw a meme where, instead of 12 roses, a man gives a woman a dozen red flags. Rich had been showing up with red flags since the minute I laid eyes on him, but, in my head, I was changing him.

We lived together, so, clearly, my old friends had been wrong.

Though we both still worked together, like most places, I was ready to move on once I could hear the rumors in the hall. I applied for a position at a different company in the chemistry lab.

I believed that once Rich and I were no longer working together, things would change.

While it was easy to place the blame on Rich for our toxic relationship, the truth was, I was just as sick. I was willing to do anything to keep it alive, changing everything about myself and my life in order to make Rich love me.

As author and thought leader Bryant McGill writes, "Toxic relationships are dangerous to your health; they will literally kill you. You were not meant to live in a fever of anxiety; screaming yourself hoarse in a frenzy of dreadful, panicked fight-or-flight that leaves you exhausted and numb with grief."

I was numb with grief, and, no matter how much I screamed, Rich refused to listen.

When I got the position at the new company, I honestly thought he would be impressed because it was a step up. But it became just another hurdle in our relationship.

"You think you're so smart," became his usual reply any time I asked where he had been the night before or who he was calling on his phone.

"You're such a fucking know-it-all, Em," he would blast me. "How about you mind your own fucking business?"

The fights would escalate until I would back down.

What else did I have?

I would go to class, come home and clean up our apartment, attending to whatever wreck had been made the night before, sleep for a few hours, and then head back to work at night. Rich and I were barely seeing each other, which seemed just fine by him.

But now, I had no one except my old friends: food and booze.

I had already started binging and purging, and, once again, it became the only thing I could control. When I got home from work, I would start drinking, waiting for Rich to join me. I couldn't keep up with my medications, so they went out the window too.

Everything began to go dark again. I felt like a drowning woman who just couldn't keep her head above water. The waves pounded me from above as the shore moved farther and farther away.

"What the fuck is wrong with you?" Rich yelled at me, waking me up to the smell of alcohol and vomit. "What are you doing?"

I could tell the alcohol was coming from Rich, but as I began to move off the bathroom floor, I realized I had passed out after I'd thrown up.

My hair wasn't falling out anymore, but it might as well have been. I was a mess.

I weighed as much as I had at 11. You could see my rib cage, and the color had once again faded from my eyes.

They say that if you don't face your trauma, you're bound to meet your perpetrator again.

I was living with mine. Every day was a different flavor of abuse, but it didn't make it less abusive.

Whether Rich was cheating on me, ignoring me, or yelling at me, I woke up scared every day. The worst part was that I wasn't scared of him as much as I was scared of being alone.

Until that morning. I don't know why. Maybe I was as horrified by me as I was by him.

Maybe I had just done this too many times before.

Maybe I could feel that there was something better out there for me, and I wasn't ever going to get it until I left Rich.

Maybe I was just sick and tired of being sick and tired.

Either way, I called my parents and told them I needed to leave. I told them I needed help looking for an apartment. They had become reasonably concerned over the last few months. Though I was in school and working, they commented on my bony appearance more than once, and, by now they had been through denial too many times not to notice the dark circles under my eyes and the sadness that emanated from me like bad perfume. I'm sure they could smell it long after I left the room.

For months, all I'd had was Rich and school and work. I was living in a bubble of binging and purging and starving myself. I was either drunk or hungover. I was always depressed.

My parents helped me get my own apartment, and though I thought it would be hard to leave, I discovered it was even harder to stay.

As soon as I left, it was like the colored lenses had been removed from my eyes, and I could see Rich as everyone else did.

Recent studies have shown that when one is experiencing romantic love, two major neural pathways associated with negative emotions become virtually shut down, preventing us from making critical assessments of the objects of our affection.

Then, when that love ends, we become acutely aware of the flaws everyone else saw.

I wanted to try again, and I was ready to stand on my own two feet, living life on my own. I finished school, graduating with a degree in chemistry and started interviewing for jobs in Portland. Though it was yet another geographic, I felt like I was ready to make good on another fresh start.

Krista, a friend from Montana, invited me to stay with her when I was in town. She happened to be living with her older brother. I drove up to the house, and he was the first person I saw. He smiled, and I was smitten.

What did I just say about standing on my own two feet and doing life on my own?

Kale had already begun building a life for himself. He had a good job and owned his own house. He was a real, live grown up, and I immediately felt like I wouldn't be good enough for him.

It took me 15 years to finally believe I was.

Chapter Eleven: Meeting Mr. Right Even if I Feel Wrong

This is the point where you would hope I would hold off on those feelings for Kale, where instead of pursuing another relationship, I would spend the time working on myself, better understanding and negotiating the parts of me that felt the need to date men like Rich or Jake or even Julian. In the end, I am so grateful that I made the unhealthy choice—even if I, Kale, and our children (another spoiler alert!), had to pay an enormous price for doing so.

I received a job offer in Portland working as a chemist at a Japanese chemical company and began spending my days in a lab as one of the few women—and the only American one—there.

After landing in Portland, I called Krista to let her know I moved to the city, and Kale answered the phone. I guess the spark had been mutual as he invited me to a party at his place that weekend. I figured there would be plenty of people there, and there were. In fact, it was a room full of dudes. My favorite.

I arrived at his place, and the two of us started drinking alongside 25 of his closest guy friends.

From that night on, we were inseparable. I would spend every day in a white lab coat, then leave work to hang out with Kale.

Since there were no women at my workplace, I didn't really have any place to make friends. Instead, I repeated the same pattern as before: adopting Kale's friends as my own and merging my social life with his.

Over the last 10 years, the term codependency has gotten used and abused, but for those of us who deal with it, the symptoms are clear. We struggle with security in our relationships. We feel uncertain or unloved. The only way to guarantee that the relationship is solid is to become hyper-vigilant, giving over our identity or getting caught up in jealousy and fear.

From the minute I met Kale, I knew I wasn't good enough. I had all this baggage, and he seemed perfect. He had a fantastic relationship with his siblings and parents. He had a great job and was happy in his work. He was part of a stable network of friends that he had for forever.

It didn't take long for me to start causing drama in his life.

I remember a conversation very early on when we were dating. We were talking about bad things that had happened to us. I told him about the rape, and, in an attempt to take a shot at honesty, I went a step further than the "rape light" story. I told him that I was young, and that it was an older boy at camp. I didn't say it was a man, and I didn't say I was 12, but it was the closest to honesty I'd ever gotten regarding that summer. I felt a small weight lifted as I waited for him to share his "bad things" story with me.

He proceeded to tell me about how his dad got fired when he was in high school. I knew that if that was the worst thing he'd ever experienced, I could never let him see the darkness my life had been. Though I'm sure it was a difficult experience, it felt light years away from rape, sex parties, and cocaine. As glad as I was to have shared, I realized I could never go any further in sharing with Kale who I had been and what had happened to me.

Like most new couples, Kale and I were infatuated with each other. He was unlike most of the guys I'd dated, with the exception of sweet Craig in high school. I felt absolutely blessed that we'd found each other, even as I also felt absolutely unworthy.

"What are you doing tonight?" Kale asked me as I talked to him on the phone in the hallway at work, whispering like a teenager talking too late at night.

"Nothing. What are you doing?"

"I was going to go to the gym. You wanna go?"

"Of course."

My heart soared as Kale and I quickly meshed our lives. We would go for long walks and do yoga together. We would meet for drinks or dinner. Weekends were spent shopping, going to concerts, traveling, or just enjoying each other's company at home. It felt like every day with each other was a vacation.

We fell head over heels very quickly.

Over the next two years, we made memories together as I slowly began to trust Kale more with who I was and how I had struggled.

One morning, lying in bed, I told him about my eating disorder.

"I ended up in a hospital in California," I explained. "I just got so sick."

"And how is it now?"

I hesitated, but I knew that Kale's sister had struggled with food as well, so I decided to be honest.

"Sometimes it's fine," I admitted. "Sometimes I throw up in your bathroom after you fall asleep."

I waited for Kale to be horrified; I waited for him to move his arm out from under my neck and say he had somewhere to be.

Instead, he pulled me in closer.

"Let's figure out how to fix that," he said quietly in my ear. "You don't need to do that anymore."

He was right. Kale brought me all the love and security I ever needed to begin to heal. Though I didn't realize it at the time, it was the love and security I should have been able to provide myself.

Kale started helping me get a hold of my eating disorder. I had shown him a peek behind the curtain; now had someone to whom I was accountable.

I was beginning to enjoy my job less and less, so Kale encouraged me to start exploring other options. I decided to pursue my master's degree in Secondary Education in the evenings in order to become a high school chemistry teacher. We both thought that teaching would be a family-friendly career, and it felt good to dream about our future together in that way.

Another big part of those early days was going out and having fun. Kale could definitely have a good time. We were both still in our 20s, heading out to bars after work and throwing parties without rebuke. As time went on, however, the booze only fueled my insecurities. And when I drank, I started projecting those insecurities on Kale.

"Do you just not want to get married?" I would ask, trying to not sound desperate, when I felt like Kale wasn't moving as quickly as I thought he should.

"No, I do," he replied.

"So you just don't want to get married to *me*!"

"That's not it, Emily. Of course, I just don't see why we need to rush things."

"I think you just want to fuck someone else, so go fuck someone else."

"What? No!" I could see the look of confusion on Kale's face. The allegation was absurd, but it was one I had been tossing around with more regularity. The fights would always escalate until I was inconsolable, convinced Kale was leaving me until, of course, he did.

It was right before my 25th birthday when Kale drove me home one night. We had gotten into a horrible fight the weekend before, but that night was innocuous enough.

He put the car in park and looked out the passenger window, just past my shoulder as he spoke.

"I don't think I can do this anymore, Emily. I just don't feel like this is working out."

I nodded, crying silently in the passenger seat. I loved him more than anyone I had ever met, but the breakup seemed to solidify what I already knew: he was too good for me.

I responded to the break up the only way I knew how. I started drinking more and starving myself.

It was a path of utter self-destruction though, thankfully, I had begun to make my own friends, leaning on them. I also had a new network of grad school classmates to soften the blow.

I was back to Square One: new city, old behaviors, same Emily.

I was so used to the cycle, I almost didn't notice when I missed my own cycle.

Then, a couple of weeks later, I started waking up nauseated. I wanted to blame my hangovers, but I knew something else was likely the cause. Though I was on the birth control patch, I found out later that it was less effective if you had a reaction to the adhesive, which prevented the medication from being transmitted properly. I, of course, fell into that category.

Three hours later, I stood in my bathroom, a positive pregnancy test in one hand, and my phone in the other.

I knew I had to tell Kale.

But I also knew that being a good Catholic boy, there would be little question about what he would want to do.

I was terrified, but I also couldn't help but hope that maybe this was the answer to my prayers. Maybe this little baby would have the power to transform everything.

"You're sure?" Kale asked, his voice shaky.

"Yes," I explained. "I've taken three tests, and it could only be yours."

There had been no one else. My doctor later confirmed as much for us both.

After meeting with the doctor, Kale said, "I love you, Emily. You know that. Maybe God just wanted to make sure we followed through on it."

I was happy to accept God's intervention in my life. I wasn't doing a very good job on my own.

We told our parents, both of whom wanted to see us get married right away.

"We want to take this slow," I explained to my parents.

My father was having none of it. "You should have taken it slow before you got pregnant," he said.

My parents had been through enough, and now here I was announcing that I was having a baby with some guy I had just broken up with a month earlier. This was on the heels of my brother announcing that his girlfriend was also pregnant.

For all they knew, Kale was another Rich.

The fact that he wasn't marrying me right away was another strike against him. The fact that my brother and his girlfriend were rushing out to get married made the situation a stark contrast to my usual domination in the favored sibling category.

But as Kale sat next to me on the couch in my parent's living room, nervously holding my hand, I knew they could tell he was doing his best.

"She's been through a lot," my dad stammered, knowing he wouldn't be able to say any more than that without getting visibly upset.

"Does he love you?" my mom asked, once Kale was out of earshot.

I didn't know how to answer that. He said he did, but I also knew that, either way, he would have stuck by me.

"He wants us to have this baby together. Isn't that enough?"

But I could tell by mom's face that it wasn't.

Kale and I went back to Portland, and, in response to both of our families, we got married that September and prepared for our baby's birth. At first, it felt really nice. We might have been playing house, but we didn't fight as much.

Unfortunately, since I was pregnant, I also had to get off my psychiatric medications. Between eating healthier, not drinking, and the blossoming relationship with Kale and the little baby on the horizon, those months were quiet and sweet.

Though it might not be everyone's experience, expecting a child brought Kale and I closer together. I no longer felt like damaged goods, dragging decades of luggage behind me. I was now Kale's wife and a soon-to-be-mother. I held tight to those identities in place of the ones I had worn over the years with other men.

Whereas everything in my relationship with anyone else had been hard, Kale and I became soft with each other, our life suddenly covered in a gauzy focus.

I continued teaching until it no longer made sense, spending my days getting our house ready for the baby's arrival.

Around the same time, my friend Erin also became pregnant. She had been my shoulder to cry on when Kale and I broke up, and one of my bridesmaids when we got married. Since we were both the first of our friends to be having babies, we became close, sharing our fears and joys as we both moved towards our due dates.

I began to believe Kale—that maybe God had done this so we would follow through with one another.

Maybe this was just how life worked—sudden, unexpected, unplanned, but tinged with impossible joy. It was a life I was beginning to embrace.

Chapter Twelve:
Building a Family

How can we ever understand the moment we become mothers? One second, we are these independent entities, free to do and mess up as we please; the next we are beholden to another spirit for the rest of our lives. We can get out of every other social contract, but the contract we make with our children is signed with our souls.

The moment Keegan was placed upon my chest, I knew everything was different.

Though I couldn't have told you what or how or even why, when I heard his first cry, every inch of my being wanted to make sure he was okay. I knew there was no going back.

I had become a mother, and my new identity was eternal.

Though Kale and I might have come together under different circumstances, we had already begun creating our own little family. For me, it was a chance to do my childhood over.

I didn't want it to just be Kale, me, and Keegan. I wanted to get out and socialize. I didn't want parenthood to stop us from enjoying our lives. It was just the beginning.

Kale and I agreed it made more sense for me to stay at home with Keegan, and I quickly got wrapped up in the accessories of parenthood.

Buying things became my main activity as I focused on presenting the best side of our sweet little family.

Keegan looked like he was dressed for a photo op every time we went out, and this was long before Instagram came around as a platform for those ops.

I was obsessed with what we looked like, and while a lot of the activities and rituals I was creating were also good for our family—arts and crafts, play dates, and music classes—they were also just another way for me to become consumed with something outside of myself.

Erin was my lifeline to the person inside, and, for the first time in my life, I developed a true and honest friendship.

We shared so much in that first year. It wasn't just about childbirth and parenting and marriages; it was about who we truly were.

One afternoon while we walked our babies around a local park, I told her the truth I had been hiding for almost 15 years. I wanted to see if I was able to say it. I wanted to see if someone would be able to hear it. And I wanted to know that I would still be able to look her in the eye after she knew.

"When I was 12, I was raped," I finally said.

The words came out so naturally. It sounded like I'd said it 1000 times though I'd never uttered that sentence in my life. Erin was shocked and upset to learn no one else knew. I told her all the details I remembered at that time, which weren't all the details I know now, but I told her that Evan was a man and about hitting my head. I told her about the shower and the maxi pads. As we made our third circle around the park, I didn't cry. That would come later, but I took perhaps the biggest step toward healing: I told the truth.

She hugged me and listened for a long time. For once, I didn't feel so alone or damaged.

I felt understood.

My life finally felt like a fit.

I wasn't taking any medications, and I felt healthy. Kale and I would go out from time to time, and we still partied a little, but it didn't feel like either of us had a problem. We were young parents who were trying to remember we were still young.

I loved being a mom, and I loved Keegan so much, I wasn't sure I wanted to jinx it with another child. We were so happy, I didn't want to disrupt anything. By the time Keegan was nine months old, Kale and I were pretty confident we were okay with having only one child. Of course, in my experience, being okay usually means you're on the brink of shit hitting the fan.

Life is funny that way. It's like you hit the top of the rollercoaster, and the view looks great. Then you take a deep breath and feel like you're living on top of the world, only to discover that the bottom is about to drop out.

Right around that time, I went to visit the doctor because I was having some irregular cramping. Because I had an IUD that suppressed my cycle, I couldn't be sure it was menstrual cramps and wanted to rule out any problems. As it would turn out, the IUD had become dislodged, and the cramping was due to the fact that I was pregnant again.

Because of the location of the IUD, removing it was the only option, which also ended the pregnancy.

That experience was hard and painful but fueled my desire to give Keegan a sibling. We wanted to try for another baby. Somehow, it felt like that was the only thing that would heal the wound of our loss.

Adding one more thing to the mix, Kale's company offered him a promotion. The only catch was that we would have to move to Pennsylvania.

At that point, it felt like it was a safe time to start anew.

For the first time, though, I wasn't running from anything I'd done wrong; in many ways, it felt like I was running towards the future.

Kale and I arrived in Pennsylvania at the start of winter. In hindsight, it might not have been the best time to move. Though my brother's marriage was imploding and my parents were wrapped in the drama of it all, I had gotten used to having family support nearby.

Now, Kale and I were all on our own.

It was also hard to leave Erin. Though we still had long talks on the phone, nothing could replace being together in person.

By the time Kale and I moved to the east coast, Erin knew everything about me and vice versa. She became the sister I never had nor knew I needed.

Now that we had landed in this new town with new people, a fresh start felt intimidating.

I started taking Keegan to a local playgroup where all my fears were allayed.

We found an amazing community in our neighborhood, and I was quickly embraced by other women. It was the first time since college that I felt part of a group.

And, just as we'd hoped, Kale and I got pregnant again. This time there was no hesitant excitement. We were thrilled. Keegan would be a big brother! We were building a family.

When Riley was born that fall, it felt as though the last puzzle piece was put into place.

We were this perfect little family of four. In fact, we were so perfect, I didn't even feel the need to prove it anymore. Kale and I loved taking road trips around the east coast with our little babies, driving up to New York to watch the leaves change colors and going to the beach in summer. We lived in an adorable town with apple orchards and pumpkin patches and rows of huge yards. It was whimsical and lovely. The love that Kale promised me when we first got pregnant felt real, and those old fears that I wasn't good enough faded even more.

We were in Vermont the following year on a vacation with our sweet little kids. I still look back at photos of that trip and remember how simple it was, and how naive I was to what was coming. It was our third anniversary, and I realized my period was late.

We had taken a "let's see what happens" approach to birth control, pretty much guaranteeing our outcome. Sure enough, I was pregnant again.

I handed a pregnancy test across the dinner table to Kale to surprise him. Surprise! He smiled, but the look on his face matched my feelings: Yay, but oh shit! Two had been perfect, but three? We were happy, but were we ready?

When Macy was born, I found out I wasn't. I couldn't feel anything. She was the loveliest, sweetest little thing, so easygoing and mellow, and I knew my feelings had nothing to do with her, but that didn't make it any better or easier.

When I looked at her, all I could muster was, "Aww, here is this cute little baby."

After years of being free from the depression that once consumed me, I could feel it filling the room again as I tried desperately to keep my head up long enough to breathe.

Chapter Thirteen:
Mental Motherhood

Target is to mothers what bars are to alcoholics: a place of calm and relief as much as it can be the site of our hardest moments.

In what seemed like a blink of an eye, I was a mother of three under three.

Kale's job kept him traveling or working at home, which meant I would have to keep the kids quiet at the house or keep them *out* of the house. Every night I was the one up with the baby and anyone else who felt like they should be awake.

I woke up every day exhausted. Often, I would find myself crunched into the glider in my daughter's room, spit up staining my clothes.

While I used to strive to always leave the house coiffed, babies matching, I was now lucky if I brushed my hair. There was only time for one of us to look good, and it was usually one of the three kids. The other two at least had on shoes (and they weren't always matching).

I was back to not eating enough. I wasn't hungry. I wasn't happy. I wasn't sad. I was just flat. Shopping and playdates became my lone comforts, along with long phone calls with my mom or Erin, waiting for Kale to come home and bring me some relief.

Motherhood can be joyous and amazing and absolutely rewarding.

But, sometimes, it's just sheer hell.

I didn't want to do arts and crafts. Getting out of the house with all three kids was an overwhelming chore. I had been changing diapers for three years without a break, and I was tired of shit and spit up. I was exhausted from breastfeeding, which I finally gave up on out of desperation.

I needed a break, but I didn't know what I needed a break from. There was nothing specific for me to be depressed about, yet I couldn't see the joy in anything. Everything was dark.

Then we went to Target.

It was the middle of August, and I had managed to negotiate the infant in the sling, my 18-month-old in the cart, and my three-year-old close enough to me to make it through the parking lot alive.

We went into the store, and, like I did any time I went out with all three kids, I prepared myself for the 40 minutes ahead, praying that everyone would behave until we made it through checkout. Who knew it would be me who was going to fall apart that day?

We were walking through the aisles when, all of a sudden, I noticed that the Halloween candy was already out. *Jesus Christ*, I thought. *Already? It's August! I need to be thinking about costumes, plans, parties?*

That's when it hit me. I would be doing this forever.

Summer. Halloween. Thanksgiving. Christmas. Easter. Summer. Repeat. Repeat. Repeat.

It was like a carousel, and I wanted off. I wanted off right at that very moment. The only problem was there was no off.

I grabbed the shelf next to me as I felt my breath constrict. I was still wearing the baby, and I was terrified I was going to faint with her on me.

I started hyperventilating. Thankfully, another customer saw me and thought I was having a heart attack. By the time the staff made it to me, I was on the floor, my toddler standing over me, my 18-month-old crying in the cart, and Macy still wrapped up in her sack as I sobbed on the floor of Target.

Postpartum depression and anxiety affect somewhere between 11 and 20 percent of women who give birth, yet most scientists have yet to understand its underpinnings. Recent studies show that there could be a biological cause for the condition—at least in some patients. It all revolves around a stress pathway in the body known as the hypothalamic-pituitary-adrenal (HPA) axis. This pathway is responsible for triggering the famous fight-or-flight response, but during pregnancy it's supposed to be suppressed to protect the fetus from stress.

One of the main drivers of this pathway is a hormone known as the corticotropin-releasing hormone, which is released by the brain during times of stress. When there is a breakdown in that pathway before or during pregnancy, the tendency towards PPD can be increased.

The fact is some of us are biologically predisposed to postpartum depression. Like most predispositions, I wasn't sure if mine was triggered by past traumas, or if, on my third child, my hormones simply met at the wrong intersection, leading me to that Target floor, overwhelmed and hyperventilating in a full panic attack while my children cried around me.

Much like my other experiences of trauma, I was deeply in my body and absolutely removed at the same time. I could see my children, but it was like I couldn't reach them.

The fear only made me breathe harder as I watched a sea of red shirts descend around me, talking to me through my tears.

They were able to get me to slow my breathing until I felt like I could stand up again.

Eventually, I was able to drive home, but after telling Kale what had happened, we agreed that something had to change.

It had been years since I had been on psychiatric medications, so I went back to a psychiatrist and started up again.

About five weeks later, on a family outing, I said to Kale, "Oh my God, I had no idea how bad I felt."

The clouds began to part. Macy started sleeping through the night, and it felt like I could breathe again. I started to fall in love with my third baby and being a mom of three began to feel more natural. Happiness returned again.

"I think I can do this," I told Kale one night after putting the kids to sleep.

Kale laughed and said, "I don't think we have a choice."

But I knew I did. I had fallen apart too many times before to think that it couldn't happen again. Kale and I started working out together in the mornings, and I was able to not only focus and function while he was at work, but I also began to enjoy my children.

Life started to feel normal, and we began to find one another again, coming out of the chaos that is life with a newborn.

Per usual, however, as soon as things got good again, I found a way to screw it up.

That winter, we went to a Christmas party and got absolutely wasted. Neither of us had been drinking much in the months prior, but we were having such a great time, we stopped looking at the clock, ignoring the number of times our glasses were filled.

Since I had been pregnant or nursing for much of the last three years, drinking had begun to feel like a thing of the past, something I did in my wild youth, but now I was a grown-up, not to mention a mother of three. I was feeling so much better, enjoying life, and alcohol just didn't seem to have a place in that life anymore.

That night, it felt like I was escaping.

But as I found out, getting drunk still came with its consequences.

The next month I found myself back in the same position I had been in three times before, standing in the bathroom staring at a pregnancy test. Here is another spoiler: it wouldn't be the last time. Whenever people ask Kale and I why we have so many kids, the question comes in many forms:

"Are there twins?"

"Are they all yours?"

"Same father?"

"Know what causes them?"

"Are you Catholic or Mormon?"

No matter the question, my response is, "We're just irresponsible!"

Not entirely true, yet that day, staring at yet another pregnancy test, I didn't feel surprise or joy. I felt nothing but fear with a healthy side of anger. I was angry with myself.

I had just come to a place where I felt balanced and right with the world, and I had immediately fucked everything up again.

This may be the point where you're pointing your finger at this book saying, "Don't you know how lucky you are? There are so many families who would feel blessed to have a child! How can you complain?" Here's the thing: we never regret the children we have. I have loved each personality, each little spirit as though they were my first. Every baby has been a blessing. But there is no doubt that in that moment, the thought of adding another mouth to feed to the three I was already barely managing overwhelmed every atom of my being. No matter how grateful we are for our children, no matter how much we see our children as blessings in our lives, mothers have the right to feel absolutely vanquished. The idea that we are supposed to feel eternally blessed every second of every day is, at the very least, unrealistic.

I was never getting off the carousel, no matter how much joy the ride gave me.

Once the shock of expecting another child wore off, life went on as usual. Things were stable and happy, and my pregnancy was fairly smooth. Unfortunately, in my third trimester, my doctor recommended that I stop taking my antidepressants.

"You can continue them as soon as the baby is born," he told me, but there had been some complications with Zoloft in late pregnancy that he wanted me to avoid.

As the summer got hotter and I got bigger and more uncomfortable, the darkness started to settle in again.

Then we took the trip from hell.

We visited Montana for a wedding, and everything went wrong. A delayed and then cancelled connecting flight left us two nights in a hotel without our luggage. The next day, my son got bitten by a tick and treated for Lyme disease, and, on the return home, my daughter dislocated her elbow in the airport on our way to the gate, resulting in an ER visit and another missed flight.

We sat in the hallway of a random, shitty hotel in Minneapolis where our kids were (finally) asleep inside. I was eight months pregnant with a 13-month old, a two-year old, and a four-year old, and I was off my psychiatric medications. I remember the day so clearly because it was all over the news that Michael Jackson had died.

I said to Kale, "After tomorrow, the last time I'm going to get on a plane with all of these kids is when we move home, closer to family."

He wholeheartedly agreed.

Though I had found amazing friends in Pennsylvania, and though I hadn't burned a single bridge there, I welcomed the thought of moving back to the Pacific Northwest.

We both had our families back on the other side of the country, and we were burning up Kale's vacation time going back and forth; it was exhausting.

More importantly, I had Erin.

We stayed in Pennsylvania until after Lainey was born. She was the sweetest, easiest baby, and for the first time since seeing that pregnancy test, I actually felt like I might survive all these children. I was back on Zoloft and life was looking up.

That's when Erin called me with the news: she had colon cancer.

I began to count the days until I could get home and be with the only person who truly knew me.

Chapter Fourteen:
Going Home

"Are you happy to be back?" Erin asked me over the phone. We had just landed in the Pacific Northwest with four children, a cat, and mountains of luggage in tow. Kale had gotten a job in Seattle, working for an aerospace company.

Erin still lived in Portland, but at least we were now in the same time zone. Just as she walked with me through my own traumas, I now had the opportunity to walk with her through hers.

I was at last strong enough for someone to lean on me, and over the next two years, as Erin went through treatments and surgeries, I felt like I was finally getting to offer her what she had always so generously given to me: unconditional love.

In a way, we all fear we might face Erin's outcome. We go in for mammograms and pap smears and skin checks knowing exactly why we are getting them, and, sometimes, we face the worst.

Cancer affects one in three women every year. It is not an illusion; it is a fact of life.

Erin was a mother with three children herself. As she struggled through treatments that seemed just as terrible as the disease itself, none of it felt fair.

At first, I wasn't sure if we were going to like Seattle, known for the "Seattle Freeze" because, unlike what I found in Pennsylvania, people aren't outwardly friendly. I don't know if it's the weather or the number of tech-focused people living in the city, but I worried I would once again be isolated, now at home with four children.

But Kale and I had each other. Alone in Seattle, we joined forces to get through it, and that first summer was so much fun. We were living out of suitcases in a tiny rental apartment that was hilariously small for a family of six. Kale was enjoying his new job, and we were getting to know our neighborhood.

Just like my parents when they moved to Helena, we were like settlers, reaching out for new ideas and new places in which to start over, to create different lives from the ones in which we were raised.

Since I hadn't drank much over the last four years, caught between pregnancies and nursing, alcohol and my issues with it felt like someone else's history. I was back on my medication, and it felt good to be settling into our new lives.

Keegan, our eldest, was about to start Kindergarten. When we were looking at schools, we found one attached to a local Catholic Church. It had a preschool as well, which was perfect.

Kale had been raised Catholic, and, when we got married, I converted. I was familiar with many different churches and religions from my years of singing and playing the flute. Though my parents believed in God, they left our faith up to us. I appreciate that to this day.

That's why, had Kale been Presbyterian, Methodist, or anything outside of a crazy cult, I probably would have converted to one of those. To me, spirituality is the most important factor; the church you join is just the club you feel most comfortable in. It's like a sorority but with more Jesus.

Whereas I was Catholic in name, Kale had been raised in the Catholic Church and its judgement and guilt. I had experienced none of that.

We found our community in that school and church. Despite the religious affiliation (or, perhaps, because of it), we quickly found that the parents liked to have fun, throwing barbeques and emptying multiple bottles of wine in the process.

That first year, we established new roots while I reconnected with my own, spending more time with my mom and Erin now that we lived only a couple hours away from them.

I would walk around our neighborhood with my triple stroller feeling healthy again. Keegan started Kindergarten, Riley began preschool, and, for the first time in years, I actually had some time to myself (at least during naptime).

Kale and I were even able to sneak away to our first kid-free weekend vacation since before we had children, thanks to nearby family and friends. We enjoyed a fun weekend in Las Vegas.

It should come as no surprise as to what happened next.

Now, I know at this point, it's almost like watching a horror movie.

"Don't go outside, Emily! Do not go outside!"

Because what happens in Vegas does **not** stay in Vegas. We ended up getting pregnant for the fifth and final time.

Here is the even crazier part: we were very happy with the news. But sometimes I wonder if the same way we came together through pregnancy, we also stayed together through it. I know that if we didn't have five children, there is a good chance our marriage wouldn't have been able to survive all the challenges that were about to come.

I often wonder if we subconsciously got pregnant, knowing it was our insurance policy against divorce—an incredibly expensive insurance policy, but well worth the baby we ultimately received.

I was four months pregnant when Erin's husband called me.

"I thought you should know, Emily," he told me with a broken voice. "She's in the hospital and isn't leaving. Hospice is here."

I had been down in Oregon the month before, and Erin and I had been able to spend time together. It was the first time over the two years she battled cancer that she looked like someone who was battling cancer: Her hat was too big for her head, her head too big for her body. She was grey from the treatments, and when her toddler came over and hugged her, I could see her wince. Everything hurt. Even hugs from her daughter.

She was one of the first I told about my pregnancy, and she responded with her usual enthusiasm, "That is so exciting! You are my joy right now. Truly."

"Oh yeah, it's going to be something. Five kids!"

"What's one more? It's perfect. It will be perfect," was her easy reply. "And it's a boy, for sure. I feel it."

That was Erin: always positive, always filled with faith.

When I said goodbye to her on that trip, tears filled my eyes.

"Don't cry," she admonished me. "I'll see you again soon."

But we didn't. She passed the same day her husband called me.

We went to her funeral a few weeks later. Her daughters were two, four, and six. I couldn't even imagine what they must have been going through, losing their beautiful mommy before they really had the chance to know her, to understand how amazing she was.

I spoke at her funeral, but I have no idea what I said. No words would have done justice to the person she was or how her loss would affect the world.

For me, Erin was the safest person I had ever met. She didn't just know my highlight reel; she knew the real me.

Five months later, the doctor would deliver our beautiful baby boy, Rowan, into my arms. Of course, Erin was right. He was perfect.

Then it hit me.

It was the first time I didn't have Erin to call. She was the first person to visit me in the hospital when Keegan was born. She was one of the first people I talked to after every baby arrived. There I was, five kids in seven years, and my confidante was gone. I was so lost without her, our long phone calls, and our easy laughter.

They say that grief can become complicated when the aggrieved can't move on. In complicated grief, painful emotions are so long lasting and severe that people have trouble recovering from the loss and resuming their lives. I couldn't accept that Erin was dead, and I didn't know how to process it. My heart was broken.

She was gone, and my secrets were gone with her.

The arc of trauma is long, and, suddenly, I felt like it was bending away from healing. I wanted a distraction, and, as if five children weren't enough, I started looking for things I did have power over, namely our highlight reel.

I had just opened an Instagram account, and I would take photos of our home and family, these amazing representations of who I wanted other people to think we were: happy, perfectly dressed, adventurous, and fun.

People would always say to me, "Wow, your hands are full."

I was so proud of the fact that my hands were full but I was handling it, and, for a long time, the photos actually matched the family. We were happy, adventurous, and fun, and we looked pretty damn good through it all.

Kale was back to working long hours and traveling, and I was handling things at home. Though chaotic and busy, I managed a happy face, even on the bad days, but, over time, the face became just that, a face. Regardless of how I felt or how things were going, to the outside world, I was the perfect modern mom, down to the blown-out curls and designer handbag.

On Instagram, I could control what people saw, but, without Erin, I once again turned to my old friend: alcohol. When I drank, my grief faded to the background. We would go to parties and out on double dates with other couples. I started drinking more socially, and it looked like how other people drank...until it didn't.

I found myself waiting with a drink in hand every night for Kale to come home. I would be overwhelmed by children and their needs; the only thing I had to look forward to was the sound of the cork coming out of the bottle.

Alcohol was my relief until it became part of my survival.

Chapter Fifteen: Projection Game

"You know those little squares aren't real," Kale laughed, looking over my shoulder as I posted another picture of Rowan on Instagram. Rowan was looking up at the phone lovingly, staring at his mommy just beyond the screen.

"I know that," I said, still finding comfort in those beautifully filtered photos, knowing they showed us at our best. That's all I wanted us to be: a family that functioned at its best.

Since we now had five children, the idea of me working had long been swept aside for full-time motherhood. This was at the height of the "Mommy Wars" in which mothers who stayed at home found themselves in an unwanted competition with the ones who worked. But, really, we mothers were in a battle with ourselves.

Though men might be historically considered the more competitive species, there is one area in which women will usually best men: the parenthood competition.

We attack it with the ambition of Olympic athletes, and I had become the Serena Williams of parenthood.

No sleep? No problem.

A baby, two preschoolers, a Kindergartner, and a second grader? You're looking at the right mom.

Three class photos and two ear infections? Get me the comb, a steamer and some antibiotics.

Five sick kids all at once? Bring it on.

Every time life threw me a curve ball, I acted like it was a homerun in the making.

But like a lot of baseball pros, I had my juice to get me through.

In the three years since moving to Seattle, our socializing escalated, which meant our drinking did as well. We found friends who liked their wine and beer, and all the parents would get together while the kids played. We acted like everything was perfectly normal because, on the surface, that's the way it looked.

I'd heard the term "Mommy juice" thrown around, but it wasn't just for mommies; it was part of the culture of parenthood. Not since college had drinking felt so normal and required for the position.

Recent research has shown that the gap between men and women with drinking problems is shrinking. Female alcohol use disorder in the United States increased by over 83 percent from 2002 to 2013, according to the National Institute on Alcohol Abuse and Alcoholism, as did alcohol-related illnesses and deaths.

#winemom became a running joke, with t-shirts and coffee cups promoting this culture we all engaged in, acting like it was normal.

I understood. Look, parenthood is hard; even more so, it can be really mundane. You can only color so many coloring books without wanting to break every crayon in half.

Grabbing a glass of wine before helping with homework or bath time became a normal routine. Since Kale had to work late most nights, or traveled, the bottle of wine was also there to keep me company. For over 10 years, that bottle had nearly faded from my life. Then, it returned with a vengeance.

"There's a great party I want to invite you to this weekend," Vanessa said, leaning across the sign in desk.

Vanessa was someone I had met at the gym and become friends with over our pregnancies. She had a wealthy husband with the car and handbag to prove it. She was well liked and well known, and her passive invite awoke something in me I hadn't felt since high school: the desire to be popular.

I called up our babysitter and though Kale was going to be out of town, I wore a tight, low-cut dress for the party.

I don't remember much from that first night out—just that Vanessa and I drank too much champagne and ended up flirting with men close to our age...but nowhere close to our set of responsibilities.

I had been living in the mommy world so long, it was like I was soaring above the canyons of another life—one where there were no children...or even a husband, for that matter.

Suddenly, it no longer mattered whether I drank or didn't drink. Everyone was just having fun, and, after five kids, I felt like I deserved it.

Rowan was almost a year old, and Kale had had a baby-making-ending vasectomy. I felt myself getting back my freedom and body.

After seven years, I could finally begin to find myself again.

I started going to book clubs, bunco nights, and girls' nights, not realizing that everywhere I went, there was a glass in my hand, not seeing the habit that had knitted itself around my life, and that of so many others.

But it was so much fun. We had a reliable babysitter, so when Kale worked, I would hit the town with Vanessa and other friends.

Vanessa was one of the few people I felt understood me since Erin had passed away. Maybe because we'd both just had our last babies. Maybe because I felt like I could be myself. Or maybe because she was dealing with her own demons in an abusive marriage to a shady, crook husband. Unlike me, while she enjoyed drinking, she had no problem stopping at one or two—a skill I could never quite perfect or understand.

We all had kids at home, but once we were at the bar, the restaurant, or the party, that all seemed to fade. Looking good was everything in this circle. It was like being in *Mean Girls* except Regina George was a 40-year old suburban housewife.

As author Rosalind Wiseman writes, "We don't leave cliques and peer pressure behind when we grow up or when we become parents, we just graduated to a new level with adults playing the roles."

I was back in the popular clique except now we threw legally-imbibed alcohol onto the fire.

With the booze came the old behaviors.

"What's your name?" a handsome man who was about 10 years younger than me asked me at a bar one evening.

The way I looked at it, I wasn't going to go home with anyone (there were five children back at my home for God's sake), so it was totally fine to flirt.

Flirting was healthy, wasn't it?

Kale liked that I was flirtatious, which I used to justify the behavior, even when he wasn't there.

Sometimes our husbands would join us, but the party didn't look much different. We just flirted with them instead and, sometimes, each other's husbands. Boundaries were a thing that seemed to go out the window when we drank.

"Am I crossing the line?" one of my husband's friends asked as he made an off-color sexual remark about me in front of everyone.

"What line?" I joked, everyone laughing at how "open and funny" we all were.

I'm not sure if it was just that so many of us had worked hard to reach this point in our lives where we had the kids and the money and the freedom to do what we wanted, but it felt like every night out was a celebration.

"We made it!" rang through every ordered margarita, every burger on the grill.

I loved that our house became a center point in all of this; it was so different from my childhood.

We had lots of friends, and we were at the center of this swirling social world.

I would take photos of us, and my friends from college and high school would remark on how amazing my life looked. I knew that some of them remembered what it had looked like before. Even as the bottle of wine at night turned into two, I became determined not to go back there, not to return to the isolation and illness that had wrecked so much of my early 20s.

My hands might have been full, but I believed I was managing it.

Until those telltale signs began reappearing, hinting that, maybe, I wasn't. I was still taking my anti-anxiety and thyroid medications regularly. My eating was normal, and I was exercising, but I began to feel weak again. When my doctor did blood work, she found that my thyroid and liver enzymes were off.

"How much do you drink?" she asked innocently enough.

I knew I should tell the doctor, but I couldn't.

"A few times a week," I lied. "Maybe more sometimes."

Always more. It was always more.

Since the medication wasn't working as well, she suggested an elimination diet.

"Removing animal proteins can be effective in people with your set of symptoms," she said, so, naturally, I decided to become vegan.

For some, veganism is a legitimate dietary choice, but, for me, it was just another way to avoid the need to eliminate alcohol. Now I was toeing the water of an eating disorder by getting rid of food groups. I became obsessive over my pursuit of a healthy diet, but, at the time, I was able to chalk it up to wellness. Besides, the doctor told me to!

Who wasn't concerned about what they put into their body? So, instead, I started putting in more alcohol.

I remember thinking more than once, *Why doesn't anyone notice how much I drink? Why doesn't the doctor ask more questions? How am I getting away with this?*

Just as I had years prior, I started spending more time with people who drank like me and less time with those who were going to question my drinking. Some of them had children, some didn't; others were divorced and only had their kids half the time.

When your acquaintances are all polishing off that second bottle at night too, no one is telling you to slow down. I knew Kale was beginning to get concerned, but I looked like I had it together, so what was he going to say?

I was busy Instagramming my fun life and making new friends. After years of stumbling through dirty diapers and breastfeeding and crying babies and inconsolable toddlers, Kale was just happy to see me focused on myself again.

The only problem was I was focusing on the wrong parts. I was like a surgeon who treated heart conditions by dying the patient's hair.

And that's what I did; I dyed my hair and got Botox and bought new clothes and matching outfits for the kids. I hired professional photographers and became determined to present the best highlight reel and, in the process, began to ignore what was real.

I ignored my health. I ignored my marriage. I ignored the fact that after years of climbing my way back up the mountain, I was cascading back into the ditch, and, this time, I had six people there to watch the fall.

Chapter Sixteen:
Mom Biz

It had been years since I'd had a job, and like a lot of life-changing events, my next career came out of a chance meeting. I asked for a skin cream recommendation on Facebook when a friend from high school responded, "I have a product you'll love."

Shelly was going to be in Seattle the following week, and we decided to go out for drinks and chat about her products. I agreed not so much because of the products but because it was a chance to drink wine. She could have been selling anything.

We met at a wine bar (the usual crime scene) where Shelly pulled out her product line and chatted with me about her business. Not only was my inner science geek impressed with the products' formulas, but I also loved that the company connected a tribe of women. They were all looking for ways to expand their own relationships with motherhood, finding themselves as wives, and strengthening their places as women.

The process of becoming a mother (anthropologists call it "matrescence") has been largely unexplored in the medical community. Researchers have traditionally studied how motherhood affects the baby, not the woman behind the birth, but a woman's story is important too. We all have a specific neurobiological experience through pregnancy and parenthood that affects our children and how we identify in the world.

We come to the job with this ideal mother in our heads. She's always cheerful and happy. She always puts her child's needs first. She has few needs of her own. Most women compare themselves against her, but they never measure up because she's not real and she never has been.

We are told it's okay to be "good enough" parents, but there is an inherent insult in the term. Since we don't know what we're supposed to be, we strive for perfection, and then hate ourselves when we fall short. Instead, we feel shame that we've fucked up as mothers.

And we keep that shame to ourselves. Even though I feel like more of us are having this conversation, it is still filtering down into action. The most "influential" mothers on Instagram continue to project a life of impossible perfection. We still show the highlight reel instead of the shit that goes on behind the scenes.

We gravitate to these pretty, easy images because the hard stuff is hard to look at—both on Instagram and in our own lives.

That night with Shelly, I realized the skincare line could not only give me a side hustle but an outlet for my identity. I was able to admit that I wasn't being 100 percent fulfilled by my kids; though I was in love with them, I needed more.

Though everything looked fine on the outside, in reality, we were just getting by.

And, more, and more, *I* was barely getting by.

"It gets me out of the house," Shelly told me that night. "I get to travel. I get to come here."

She was offering me everything I had been looking for.

We clinked glasses of wine as I saw my own possibilities.

I wanted to travel. I wanted to find a way to help my family. Perhaps, more than anything, I wanted another job title outside of mom.

The upside of the job was that it involved selling a product I actually used and believed in...all over drinks.

Inviting people to wine was part of the deal, and it quickly became a part of mine. Now I didn't even have to feel guilty when I went out drinking. It was my job!

Still, I knew that some of my behaviors weren't "right." I knew that when I brought a bottle of wine up to the bathroom, pouring a glass before I got in the shower—and another when I stepped out—that I was pushing a line. And as I watched that number on the scale tick down to a level I hadn't seen since before I'd had five kids, I knew I probably wasn't being smart with my new vegan lifestyle either.

There were so many little clues littering my trail, but it was easier to head to book club with a bottle of wine in my bag and not have to see what was becoming a litany of bad decisions.

I would wake up the next morning and see the evidence in my text message history or on Facebook—dumb stuff I had posted or written. I would delete it all with a cringe in my stomach, knowing how many people read it before I did.

Though I would wonder why no one was confronting me on my drinking, the fact is, they were noticing. They were also affirming my decisions.

They would laugh about the things I did because, once again, I was the fun girl.

"How funny that you passed out after playing beer pong. Cute!"

"So hilarious that you threw up after taking those shots. You're fun!"

"You adorable little flirt; look how you sit on my husband's lap! Aren't you just the coolest?"

I was the mom everyone wanted to party with. For some people, it was because I made their drinking look better; for others, a night out with me felt like something exotic.

I understood. I had escaped once too, but now I was free.

Or so I believed.

I kept bottle openers stashed throughout my house – in the bathroom, in the laundry room, one was always in my purse – so I could sneak away to drink while my kids ate dinner or played in the backyard.

I would post photos of me doing arts and crafts with my kids, but no one could smell the alcohol on my breath or hear the slight slur in my voice. Kale was too busy to notice. When he was around, we were usually spending time with friends, sitting around our backyard, all with beers in our hands.

We would make margaritas and tacos and watch Seahawks games. Some nights we went out for martinis with a group of friends. We took family vacations together. The wine would flow, the beers would be uncapped, and our kids would play.

"I think I'm going to only drink when we have friends in town," I told Kale one night as we got ready for bed.

"Are you worried about your drinking?" he asked after a brief pause.

"No," I lied, hoping he didn't find the bottle opener under my vanity sink. "I'm just thinking for health reasons."

He kissed me on the forehead before pulling back the comforter. "Sounds good. I could probably stand to cut down too."

I nodded my head, but then, a few days later, when friends invited us over to their house, quitting drinking all of a sudden seemed like such a silly idea. So what if I had wine by myself? Drinking wine at night was perfectly normal.

Besides, drinking was a key part of my business, which was growing quicker than I ever imagined. My social networks were giving rave reviews of my products, and business was booming. Soon, I was earning praise and promotions at work for my sales figures.

I loved working with other people. After years of being home and talking to children all day, I loved getting to be amongst adults, particularly other women who were busy managing the balance between wifehood, motherhood, womanhood, and humanhood.

Once again, it was work, drink, party, drink—a very old but familiar cycle. Only now I was parenting in between it all.

Kale and I would spend many evenings with friends around the outdoor fireplace, a frequent backdrop for our parties. One of these friends, Stephen, had recently become single. He was spending more time around our house, whether for help, or advice, or company. He shared stories of his new bachelor life that always made us laugh, and possibly led us to yearn for that same freedom again ourselves. The thing was, Kale wasn't always around. He would be working late as Stephen and I texted or chatted.

"Thanks, Em," Stephen said one evening, standing dangerously close to me as he got up to leave.

I could feel my breath catch in my throat, but I tried to ignore it. No matter what was going on, I was married. Stephen was just a friend. I knew the last thing I needed to do was give in to some passing flirtation.

Until I didn't.

Chapter Seventeen:
Blurred Lines

You always think the affair starts the minute you land in bed with a stranger on top of you.

But the affair started way before that, maybe even before Stephen and Kale and I became friends.

Maybe it started that first night I went out with Vanessa and felt like it was no big deal to flirt with other men because it wasn't like I was going home with them.

Maybe it started decades before when I decided that sex wasn't love, and love wasn't sex.

I knew that Stephen's presence wasn't the healthiest. Here he was, a single man, reaching out to me for companionship. And though we always stood on opposite sides of the kitchen island, opposite sides of the couch, opposite ends of the phone, we found ourselves wanting to be around each other more. Still, I didn't see the closeness sneak up on us.

That was the thing about the affair: A lot of people use affairs to escape their marriages, but I was actually happy in mine. I didn't see the warning signs.

A few months prior, Kale and I had enjoyed a week-long vacation in Mexico without the kids. We had an amazing week. It felt like when we first met, back when every day together was a vacation.

The only downside to our week in Mexico was how my body was responding to the alcohol. Since we were kid-free, we drank a lot, but I started to experience some odd consequences. After a night of drinking and feeling buzzed but not blackout drunk, I woke up the next day throwing up, shaking, and with a fever. I assumed I'd eaten something bad or drank something nasty in Mexico, but then, by the next evening, once I started drinking again, I felt better. This happened the next day and the next. I wasn't sure if I was experiencing withdrawals, but I felt like I was losing control over my drinking and how it made me feel.

I was in the middle of building my presence on social media, so it's no coincidence that it was ultimately one of those pictures from the trip that lit the flame between Stephen and me.

Kale took a photo of me in my bikini, which I then posted to Facebook.

Months later, someone must have mentioned it to Stephen, who didn't have Facebook. One random day, Stephen texted me: "Throw me a bone...I'm missing out! Send me that bikini pic I've been hearing about on Facebook."

I don't know why I did it. At the time, I tried to pretend it was an innocent request, justifying it because I was sharing a photo that I had already posted for the whole world to see.

How could that be wrong?

The minute I sent it, though, I went back into my texts and deleted it.

Trust is fragile; once the lie begins that you can't rein in, it becomes emotional wildfire, burning through everything, damaging relationships, sometimes irreparably. For me the lies had always been there—from the white lies to the fibs I had been telling myself for decades. But as I was just beginning to learn, honesty was about more than just not lying; it was also about showing my partner who I was. Otherwise the lies become so big, you start to believe them yourself.

The thing was, I had already been lying to Kale for years. The lies weren't the words I told him; they were the words I didn't.

He didn't know how severe the drinking and drugging had been. He didn't even know the full truth about my past traumas. He didn't know who I really was, so it was easy for me to believe that someone else might be better at knowing me.

Deleting a text seemed like the right thing to do. I wasn't getting rid of evidence; I was protecting Kale from an innocent mistake.

Then the mistake became a lot less innocent. The minute the text was sent, it felt like I set off a row of dominos.

Stephen replied, "Thanks. You're smoking hot."

With that volley, we suddenly crossed whatever vague line we had tried to draw.

The text messages quickly began to pile up from there:

"I wish I had met you 20 years earlier."

"I wish my husband gave me this much attention."

"I wish we could run away right now."

Finally, it was like, "Why wait? Why not run away right now?"

There is a passion that can only be created in the forbidden. That is why affairs are so intoxicating and why they can go on for so long. They are false fantasies, carried on outside of reality without combined bank accounts, children, laundry, or any other responsibilities.

No matter how hard you might try to turn up the heat with your own spouse, you have already exchanged vows. Assuming you're in at least a reasonably happy marriage, you're not making a mistake when you sleep with your husband. An affair, on the other hand, is an incredibly addictive mistake, and I had a long history of making mistakes.

A few months earlier, Stephen had been like any other guy I knew. Now he was a new escape. A new addiction.

Not long after the bikini picture, I met Stephen at his house, crossing a line neither of us ever intended to cross, and we continued to cross one line after another, even as the stakes grew higher.

We would try to arrange dinner parties and barbeques and events as families or groups of friends just to see each other. Through it all, the tension was so thick you could cut it with a knife.

Of course, the whole thing was fueled by alcohol.

Those weeks turned into months and became a blur as I drank to escape with Stephen, as I drank to cover up my indiscretions with Kale, as I drank to submerge my own guilt.

The lie had become too big; it overwhelmed everything I did. I lived in fear and, at the same time, anticipation. It felt like I had committed murder. I had killed the most sacred thing between Kale and I, the one thing that held our whole family together: our trust.

I know this is the part where I come off looking like a terrible mother and wife. I know this is the part where you might be shaking your head, thinking I'm a horrible woman and human.

I know this is the part that is easy to judge and to hate.

I know, because I hated myself so much at that point, I wanted to die.

That old story, that Kale was this perfect, wonderful man, and that I would never deserve him, came back in full force.

I mean, how could it not?

Here I was running around with our mutual friend behind his back. Here I was lying to his face and sneaking around our children.

I was watching the same story unfold that you are now reading, and I couldn't stand the main character. She had everything, yet she was risking it all for…what?

For an affair?

For a man who probably could have cared less for her?

For her own selfish despair?

While I hated myself, I also knew I wasn't a bad person. I was just broken. I had been broken for a long time and I had made it look so good on the outside, I nearly believed it myself. The truth was, everything inside had begun to rot.

Marriage is a promise, but it is one we make real. We build houses on that promise. We bring children into it. We create bonds we hope will last us until our last breath, holding our beloved's hand as they slip into eternity.

I knew that in order to keep my promise, I had to be honest. I had to tell Kale the truth. I didn't know what the outcome would be, but it had to be better than the feeling I was carrying around with me every day.

But every time I had the chance to say something, the words failed to come.

I knew the lies were decaying everything that was good inside me, yet I couldn't quit.

Chapter Eighteen: The Heartbreak of Affair

It took me a few more years to understand that I had spent most of my adult life getting high from things—whether it was alcohol, starvation, clicks on Instagram, or a full-blown affair.

I couldn't see how every time I took a drink or threw up or hooked up with a guy, I was checking out of reality. Even as my relationship with Stephen deepened, I couldn't understand that it wasn't Stephen I was interested in, it was the rush of the lie.

It was no different than when I was eight, exaggerating sprinklers into Slip-n-Slides.

It was no different than when I was 15, stealing someone's boyfriend.

It was no different than when I was 17, pursuing a guy I knew was dangerous.

It was no different than when I was 18, stealing money from the till.

It was no different than when I was 19, hanging out with seedy people and snorting coke.

And so on, and so on, throughout my entire history.

The adrenaline of getting away with it would remove me from my present. The heartbreaking part was that I actually loved my present situation.

I loved my husband and my children. I loved them to my core.

There is a line in the big book of Alcoholics Anonymous that reads, "Hitting bottom is losing the one thing you love most, and still refusing to quit."

I knew how much was on the line every time I saw Stephen text, and I still snuck away to respond.

Some neurologists call this "flame addiction," the chemical and hormonal changes that take place when someone is engaged in the forbidden. During infatuation, the brain produces neurochemicals that can alter one's reality; the rush of adrenaline-like norepinephrine can take one's breath away, literally. Then, when the source of infatuation goes away, the brain experiences a significant decrease in serotonin, creating a sense of emptiness and an obsessive preoccupation with that person.

Every time I was communicating secretly with Stephen, it was like I was taking a hit of the best drug on the planet. When he was gone, I found myself in withdrawal.

I knew what was at stake—not just my marriage, but my children. My whole world. Even so, I just couldn't stop myself.

With the affair, I had reached a new "low." I had broken so many rules, it seemed like no rules were worth honoring anymore.

I mean, I've crossed so may lines, what does it matter if I flirt with a guy at the bar? I thought. *Who cares if I text back another dude?*

As long as I wasn't sleeping with them, I figured, my behavior couldn't be that bad.

I had lowered the bar so much that my judgement was altered. It wasn't that I lost my moral compass, but that North had become South. East was now West.

Boundaries became pointless, and standards were lost—much like justifying drinking in the morning because it's a mimosa or hanging out with friends who cosigned my bullshit so they didn't have to look at themselves.

I was a bad woman doing bad things, and I couldn't find my way back to normal, let alone good.

They say you create self-esteem when you do esteemable acts.

Likewise, you lose esteem when you do naughty ones.

My life had become one of overcompensation where vanity and "how things looked" trumped authenticity and "what things were."

I was drinking more than ever, assuring that I would continue to make bad decision after bad decision. I couldn't stand myself, and I couldn't imagine what would happen if people knew what was really going on. Nobody does something this horrible, do they?

In fact, they do. Studies find that more than one in five Americans have an affair, and that women are now about as likely as men to cross the line. In a recent University of Vermont study, 98 percent of the men and 80 percent of the women reported having a sexual fantasy about someone other than their partner at least once in the previous two months.

Infidelity is a part of more marriages than people want to admit. Roughly 20 percent of marriages experience infidelity, yet only nine percent of married people admit to cheating.

Of course, I wasn't thinking about any of these stats when I was in the middle of my own affair. It felt like days and weeks were running into each other. I didn't know how to make it stop though I could see the train was about to go off the tracks.

Stephen and I both knew it needed to end. I understood that Stephen wasn't part of the plan for my future. I had no intention of leaving my family. But I also didn't know how to say no.

There was no doubt in my mind that Kale loved me. There was no doubt in my mind that I loved him. But I was still plagued by the feeling that I wasn't good enough for him. I didn't feel that he needed me, and my own behavior was only cementing that fact in my brain. I felt so needed by Stephen. Even though that need was toxic and irrational and had no place in reality, I didn't know how to say goodbye to it, and the escape from the chaos of my life, the carousel that I couldn't get off, was too comforting to let go.

I was paralyzed. I was back on the ground staring up at the sky. I didn't say no, but I didn't say yes.

I needed an intervention, but I wasn't sure how to make it happen. I think when we can't consciously make a decision, our subconscious eventually does it for us.

In my case, the phone did the talking for me.

"Are you having an affair with Stephen?"

I was half awake when I heard the question. As usual, I'd had a few glasses of wine at dinner and wasn't entirely there when I woke to Kale standing above me.

"What?" I asked. Kale was holding my phone.

"Are you having an affair with Stephen?"

My mind whirled as I tried to remember what he could have possibly found. Missed calls? Photos? Text messages. Yes. Text messages.

Though I was back to blacking out, I could remember the exchange clearly—Stephen writing that he wanted to see me, me replying that I couldn't wait to see him.

I had been lying for so long, the truth fell out of me like this enormously unbearable weight.

I sat up in bed and looked my good, kind husband in the eyes: "Yes."

What happened next was an even bigger blur. My usually calm husband lost his mind, throwing my phone against the wall and screaming at me.

"How could you, Emily?"

Then, with an equally sudden force, he headed downstairs, screaming, "That motherfucker!"

By the time he made it to the front door, keys in hand, it was too late. He was gone.

As I later found out, he drove to Stephen's house in the middle of the night, rang the doorbell and punched him squarely in the face.

Stephen tried to talk to him and reason with him, but there was nothing to talk about or reason with.

By the time Monday rolled around, word had gotten out. It was a hot button topic. I knew the sound of those whispers. I had been hearing them my whole life. But they meant nothing in comparison to Kale's silence.

"I just want to know," he asked me the next afternoon, "How long has this been going on?"

It was a question I didn't know how to answer. Again, it was easy to blame the photo, that one stupid text that started it all, but the affair had really begun decades before, when a 12-year-old walked into a forest and came out a different person.

I didn't want to use the story as an excuse, but I also knew that I owed it to Kale to tell him the truth—not just about Stephen, but about me.

"I've just been fucked up all my life. But I want to get better, Kale, I do."

I was so tired of this dance—of rebuilding only to fall apart.

It was a terrible cycle, and every time I thought I was doing better—getting on medication, controlling my eating disorder, stabilizing my drinking—I always ended up taking two steps back. As much as I tried to move forward, my progress always returned me here, to this place I never wanted to visit again.

And, now, it wasn't just about me or Kale, it was about this big, wonderful life we had built. I couldn't keep risking its safety because I refused to heal.

I couldn't even blame Evan anymore; the shame had become all mine.

Over the next few months, Kale and I would try to heal our marriage, going to marriage clinics and counseling. I tried to do damage control socially, addressing gossip as best as I could with people who seemed more interested in my life than their own. Surprisingly, I was also fighting off advances from other men who now saw me as an easy target.

What was even more surprising was the number of women who started coming to me to tell me about their marriages.

The women who I thought were the most judgmental, the uppity Queen Bees I thought would be keen to cast the first stone, pulled me aside and confessed that they had done the same. There were also those who judged, many of whom later came out of the woodwork to confess the same thing had happened to them. Our whole story was out there, and we had to accept it, but another surprising gift emerged: through our public pain we were able to help others confront what they had done in private. It wasn't just healing for them, it was healing for us as well.

As Shauna Niequist writes in *Present Over Perfect,* "What people think about you means nothing in comparison to what you believe about yourself."

It's easy to say, "Not me, not my marriage." I had once said the same, up until the exact moment I sent that first deleted text. I was the first person to ask, "How could this have happened?" Now, I truly believe the only people who are immune to affairs are those who understand it is possible for them to happen.

The whole time I was having an affair, I believed I was alone. Even as I write this, even as I know that it will potentially wound my husband again, I have to share it for all the women out there who think they're alone too.

Affairs don't happen in a vacuum, and, ultimately, as much as I had to own my side of it, Kale and I couldn't heal until we could begin to trace my infidelity back to the DNA of our relationship.

Our decision to get married in the face of pregnancy… Kale's dedication to his work that left me feeling alone and isolated... Our choices throughout our marriage—both the ones that supported and the ones which neglected the trust we had worked so hard to build...all of it had a piece in this puzzle.

Affairs thrive in secrecy, so Kale and I had to end our secrets.

That work wasn't easy. It took place in fits and starts as we tried to find a new love language between us, one which better communicated our emotional needs.

Our relationship had been born out of survival, and survival is no place for love to flourish.

In order to rediscover that commitment, in order to restore our trust, I had to do more than not lie; I had to be honest about who I was.

I wish I could say I was willing right away, but I had been telling lies my whole life. Truth was an uncomfortable place, and I wasn't quite ready for it.

Chapter Nineteen:
Fallout

Once the affair was discovered, I was thrust back into real life. I was back in a world of dirty dishes and marriage and money and whether or not we were going to survive this.

"Emily, do you want to stay married?" our marriage therapist asked. She was an older woman with thick glasses.

I smiled nervously. I knew what I was supposed to say. Of course I did. I was the one who'd had the affair after all. If I wanted to save my marriage, I needed to act like I wanted to be there. But it was hard to be in two places at once, and I still hadn't been able to entirely stop communicating with Stephen.

Though we no longer saw each other, the text messages continued in secret, and though there was nothing sexual or romantic about them, the stakes were higher than ever before.

I was back to wanting it to end, but the drug was too strong.

I could either stare at the dirty dishes, or I could enjoy the fantasy.

The only problem was that even the fantasy was beginning to tarnish.

The rose-colored lenses through which I had viewed Stephen throughout our affair began to change. What used to be sexy was beginning to feel weird.

But like any drug, even when it stopped working, I didn't know how to quit.

I had to start telling the truth somewhere, and marriage counseling was as good of a place as any. So I began to talk.

Instead of just telling Kale I was fucked up, I told him why.

I told him about Evan. The real story. That I was 12 and he was a full-grown man.

I told him about all the times I had gotten drunk and cheated on other boyfriends. I told him about all the times I had gotten drunk and made other bad decisions.

Now, you might think at this point that one of us might have started flagging "getting drunk," but we focused on other problems—namely how hard it was to be home alone all the time with five kids.

"Kale," the therapist explained. "Emily gave up her career to stay home with the kids. Now, she had the opportunity to pursue her own goals, yet all the children's needs are still on her plate. It's important for both of you to figure out a way to make that work."

Kale was being forced to process all this information—the affair and my trauma and my own bad decisions—and now he had to do all this stuff on top of it, like work less and take care of the kids more.

Our solution: we hired a live-in au pair.

In retrospect, that probably wasn't the solution to healing our relationship, but it at least gave us some space to try.

I loved being a mother, but there was no doubt that parenting five children alone most nights had begun to take its toll. It was no excuse for my affair, but I didn't even know how to carve out the time to grow.

And it was time for me to do more than grow; it was time for me to grow up.

Although I had learned how to juggle five kids, although I paid the bills and acted like a grown up, I had never really done the work to get out of my own adolescence.

Between my party life and my friends and my drinking, I acted like an overgrown teenager who didn't know how to take responsibility for her actions.

This concept of extended adolescence is nothing new. It was first made famous by psychologist Erik Erikson. In his theory on the different stages of human development, he termed this stage a "psychosocial moratorium."

Often young adults experience this phenomenon as they suspend responsibilities and commitments in search of their new identities.

In my search to discover who I was, I had ignored the commitments that meant the most to me.

In a way, I had been in a psychosocial moratorium since the age of 12, and my drinking wasn't making it any better. When Rowan was about two years old, he found a champagne glass and brought it to me because that's what he associated me with.

That is what all my children knew of me. I was fun and funny, and we all had a good time, but Mommy always did so with a drink in her hand.

Our kids could see it even if Kale and I couldn't.

It was just like the rose-colored glasses through which I saw Stephen: if your eyes are veiled to the truth, you'll create a different reality.

The reality Kale and I were living in was one in which, as long as I had some help and he came home a little earlier, we might make it through.

"Do you think that's enough?" our therapist asked, peering over her glasses. "You know marriages usually don't get to this place just because Dad works a little late."

I knew she was right. Finally, Kale forced me to come clean.

"You haven't stopped texting Stephen," he accused. "I know you haven't."

"You're right," I shamefully admitted.

I could see the sucker punch to Kale's gut. Here we were trying to do all these things to make it better, and I still hadn't disengaged with the very problem that had made it so wrong in the first place.

"Why?" Kale asked desperately.

"I don't know," I cried. "I don't know."

In that moment, though, it didn't matter that I didn't know. All I knew was that I was exhausted from all the work we were putting into our marriage, only to undermine it with furtive text messages.

I wanted to do this right.

The next day, I deleted everything, including Stephen's number. I did what I should have done weeks prior: I completely severed the relationship. I needed to concentrate on my marriage.

And I did. Kale and I began to focus on each other, maybe in a way we never had before. That said, even as our marriage started to get better, my drinking failed to improve.

Now that Kale and I had hired a live-in au pair, it was even easier to get away.

I was travelling with my business and becoming even more successful.

The au pair gave me the freedom to focus on my career and my marriage, but she also gave me the freedom to drink however I wanted.

Now I wasn't just drinking away past traumas; I was drinking away my days and nights.

I was quickly realizing that being embarrassed from drinking doesn't stop you from drinking—in fact, quite the opposite. In a study of alcoholics and relapse rates, researchers found that the more shame-ridden a drinker looked when talking about drinking—hunched shoulders or failing to look the interviewer in the eye—the person was more likely to relapse and to drink even more than before.

Shame is not only an effect of addiction but also can be a key reason why some people drink or use drugs in the first place. Research suggests that people who feel particularly high levels of shame are at an increased risk for addictions and other conditions that can worsen addictions, like depression.

That can set up a vicious cycle: If you drink to escape shame and then embarrass yourself while drinking, you wind up with even more reasons to drink—and to be ashamed of yourself.

Despite all the shame and drinking, there were still so many moments when my family and I were happy. If everything had been terrible all the time, I would have known what to do. The hard part was that there were so many successes alongside my mistakes and bad behaviors: all the wonderful, fun adventures where everything felt just right, all the afternoons spent with me and my kids, even the beginning of a new, burgeoning trust between Kale and me.

Then, just when I began to feel like we were moving on, we were struck by another setback.

Chapter Twenty: Filtered Life

I sat across from my doctor in her office. You know it's never good news when you're sitting across the desk from a doctor. Only bad news is reserved for those kinds of conversations.

I swallowed the word hard. "Cancer?" I asked.

"Yes," she began to explain. "But, look Emily, the procedure is simple, we'll have you up and running in no time. We caught it early and that's the most important part."

Cervical cancer was once the most fatal type for women, but with the development of the pap smear, those numbers have plummeted. I knew there was a good chance I would be fine, but it was scary to face nonetheless.

Thankfully, the surgery was a success, and, as I left the hospital after, the nurse gave me a prescription.

"What's this for?" I asked.

"For the pain," she explained, "It's what you've been taking in the hospital."

I had quit drinking before the surgery because my doctor warned me that it could cause complications during the procedure and my healing process.

Now I had something even better.

Kale filled my prescription for Vicodin that day, and, by nightfall, I was feeling a calm I hadn't experienced in years.

I felt relieved of everything—the burden of the affair, the burden of the surgery, and, now that I wasn't drinking, the burden of alcohol.

The thing I didn't realize was that the alcohol had begun to stop working. Though I was still drinking at night—slipping off to the kitchen to refill a glass that never seemed to empty—I could still hear the thoughts in my head, I could still feel the pain in my chest.

The Vicodin erased both. Like many Americans, I knew about the opioid epidemic, but that sounded like something that happened to other people like the strung-out homeless who gathered on corners downtown, not a successful mother of five.

As I burned through my prescription, I figured that would never happen to me.

I had spent my whole adulthood addicted to something, yet I somehow still believed I was immune.

How's that denial for you?

As the last pill slid into my hand, I tried to think about how I could get more. I could tell the doctor I was still in pain though I knew that would only precipitate a doctor's visit. I wondered how I might otherwise get more. I rifled through our medicine cabinet, curious if we had any old painkillers that I didn't know about. I started racking my brain about which friends recently had had surgeries and might have their own stash of drugs. I had been given one prescription and was already trying to figure out how to break the law to get more.

I knew the slippery slope I would be headed down, and though I was heading towards a new bottom, I decided to use my old vehicle: alcohol. If I couldn't keep the Vicodin going, at least I still had my wine.

Now it felt like I really couldn't stop. I would wake up and hear my children downstairs with Kale, unable to remember what had happened the night before. I was travelling for work and would frequently come to in my hotel room, unsure how I had gotten there.

Despite my blackouts, I was hitting all my sales goals and beginning to garner recognition with my company. I was being asked to speak at events and was even being used in marketing materials.

Within a matter of years, I had moved from a rookie consultant to top earner. That little Instagram profile I'd started had blown up, influencer style. I had never intended to be an influencer and couldn't help but laugh at how far from the truth my highlight reel felt.

There in those little squares was the life I wished we were living: a happy marriage, a healthy wife, a happy motherhood. Behind the scenes, however, we were barely surviving.

That summer, I earned a brand-new luxury SUV for hitting a sales milestone. My colleagues and I had a big presentation and celebration the day I earned it, and I spoke in front of a crowded room about our company and about how much the work had meant to me.

None of it was a lie.

My business had brought a dimension to my life that had been completely missing. I got to build a community of women all trying to navigate their lives who found a common language through health and beauty.

And I was completely wasted for all of it.

When I was done presenting, I kept drinking, glass of champagne after glass of champagne.

I don't remember leaving the hotel. It felt like the night was slashed into pieces.

I got behind the wheel of that shiny new SUV and left the event. It wasn't until I saw the red and blue lights flashing behind me that I realized I shouldn't have been on the road.

My whole life was turning into one big shouldn't have.

I shouldn't have married Kale.

I shouldn't have dragged him into my shit.

I shouldn't have cheated.

I shouldn't have been a mother of five kids with red and blue lights flashing behind me, yet there I was, feeling the cold metal cuffs slide onto my wrists just as they had years before when I got arrested for stealing.

I didn't argue; I didn't even cry.

I felt the same way as when I woke up with Kale standing above me, asking if I was having an affair.

I was defeated.

After getting to the police station, I was taken to the lobby where I was allowed my one phone call. I picked up the receiver with a shaky hand.

I called Kale, but he was asleep and didn't answer.

I called my colleague Sarah who had just left the event herself. She found someone sober to drive her to the police station to pick me up and take me home.

By then, it was morning. I walked into our bedroom where Kale was sleeping. "Kale," I said, trying to keep my shit together. I was reminded of when my mother came to pick me up at music camp. I wanted to cry in his arms. I wanted to tell him I was ready for it to end, that I was so embarrassed and ashamed and so, so sorry.

But I didn't. I just told him I got a DUI. He hugged me and said he was so sorry it happened. He told me to get some sleep.

"I've got the kids today," he assured me, positive as always. "We will get through this; it will be okay."

I wasn't so sure.

I went through the motions of taking care of the DUI. I got my car out of impound, applied for a restricted license, hired a lawyer, and had a breathalyzer placed in that shiny new SUV.

Every time I would take my kids to school in the morning, any time I had to start the car, I would have to blow into the breathalyzer for it to start. The only problem was if I had drunk too much the night before, I would still blow a high enough BAC (blood alcohol concentration) for the car not to start.

Yes, you read that right.

Even after the affair, even after the DUI, even after the breathalyzer that I would need to pass in order to get my kids to school, I couldn't stop drinking.

I wanted to so badly, but I still felt like that wasn't really the problem. The problem was that I wasn't showing everyone else what a problem it was.

I had a court order to receive a drug and alcohol evaluation. Even then, even when talking to a professional, I lied about my alcohol use.

As my court appearances and fines were taken care of, one by one, I found out how common DUI's actually were.

More than one million people, I learned, are arrested every year for driving under the influence. That statistic made me feel better. I lived off justifying statistics.

These are the statistics that didn't make me feel better: Every day, on average, 28 people die because of drunk driving crashes. In 2010, people killed in alcohol-impaired driving crashes accounted for nearly one-third (31 percent) of all traffic-related deaths.

Friends started calling me as soon as they found out, sharing stories of their own DUIs or near-bust experiences. It seemed like everyone had gotten pulled over for drinking and driving at some point.

Maybe it wasn't a problem after all but, rather, a rite of passage.

With each supportive text message, I felt less guilty about my own bad decisions, justified by their comradery, even as I went back into the house and asked the nanny to drive our kids to school because I couldn't get the car to start.

In the meantime, I kept posting inspirational quotes and pretty pictures of our life and home. I filtered everything so deeply, even I couldn't see the truth.

Kale and I had only just started to make our way out of the other side of the affair and here I was hitting another rock bottom.

I wondered how many more I could possibly hit until I found out there is always one more.

Chapter Twenty-One:
The Lowest Bottom

Here we return to the beginning and, in some ways, the end. I was waking up every day with so much guilt, so much shame. Between Stephen and the DUI, it felt like I just couldn't get it right. I was still excelling at work, but it was like when I was a kid playing the flute without having to practice. I was hitting my numbers without trying that hard.

They say that imposter syndrome comes when you don't feel you deserve the life you have. I felt like I was cheating at the game. I had cheated in my marriage; now I couldn't even enjoy the successes I was experiencing at work.

I was numb to everything.

One night I went out for another celebration at work. I took a cab home, but Kale was horrified by my state.

He shook his head like a disappointed father.

"I can't keep doing this with you, Emily. I just can't keep living on this roller coaster."

I understood; I couldn't either.

We fought though I can't remember the details of why. Maybe I'd been caught flirting. Maybe I got too drunk and posted something inappropriate on social media. You never knew. But the theme of the argument was basically everything I'd done to fuck up our lives.

I was beyond exhausted. I felt like I was back in college, avoiding my eyes in the mirror, unable to accept who I had become.

I stopped being able to hold it together with the kids. I started making them late for school, forgetting to send lunches or field trip forms. I could hear the whispers in the hallways again, but it was different this time. This time, it was my children talking to each other. They were starting to catch on to who their mother was.

I couldn't continue to be a ghost in my own home, and I believed with my whole soul that everyone wanted me gone. I knew Kale was ready to move on; I had put him through enough.

That night, after everyone had gone to bed, already a bottle deep, I walked into the bathroom where I had a bottle of champagne stashed in the closet and closed the door behind me. I walked over to the medicine cabinet, pulled out a bottle of sleeping pills, and slid down against the tub.

I loved my children as much as I had back in the delivery room, holding each of them in my arms for the first time, but I also believed they would be better without me.

I would be saving them the pain of me being their mother.

I opened up my phone and found those pictures, the ones I posted to show how perfect we were. Then I slid the bottle of pills to my lips and swallowed the first mouth full, chasing it with champagne.

Gulping back my tears, I swallowed another round of pills, emptying the prescription bottle before I threw it against the bathroom mirror, drinking the rest of the bottle.

I texted Kale what I thought would be my last words:

I never meant to hurt you. I'm an awful broken person. I've been living in my own prison for so long and I just want out. There is so much you don't know and I don't want to burden you with. You deserve so much better. I'm so sorry I couldn't be that for you. I've tried so hard to get better and improve myself and be the wife you want me to be but I just don't know how to be normal. I'm so sorry. You are such an amazing husband and person and father. You will be better off without me — so will the kids and our friends and everyone. Just know that I love you and the kids so so so much. More than anything in the world. All I ever wanted was to be your wife and be a mom and I couldn't even do that well. I'm so sorry I couldn't be better. I keep screwing up and I probably would continue to. I just don't know how to be normal. I do know that I can't do this life without you. I just can't. You are my lifeline. I can't bear to look at the kids in the eyes anymore and see their disappointment and know it's all my fault. Let the kids know I love them so much, I know you will do what is best for them as you are the very best dad ever. Please tell them they are the best things that ever happened to me. You are too. I love you so much. You will all be happier without me, please find happiness now that you are free of me hurting you all the time. I love you and I'm so sorry.

I clicked send and got into bed with Kale. I didn't know what the outcome would be. I didn't know if I would ever see my family again. There was such a huge part of me that honestly believed I was doing them a favor. Then everything went dark.

I didn't know that Kale rolled over and saw his phone light up, read the text message and rushed into our bathroom where he found the empty bottle of champagne and pills.

I didn't hear him screaming as he called 911, carried me to the car, and raced us to the hospital, calling my name the whole way.

I didn't know they would manage to get me to throw up once I got to the hospital, before I slipped back to sleep, finally waking up to IVs in my arm and my husband asleep in the chair next to my hospital bed.

"Kale," I croaked.

Kale nearly jumped, as though he thought I was already dead. He grabbed my hand. "Emily! Thank God. Thank God."

I didn't know why he was grateful I was alive, but a small part of me was too. I was grateful to find myself in that bed. I was relieved to see Kale sitting beside me.

Just like the DUI, I wasn't alone in my suicide attempt. Suicide is the 10th leading cause of death in the US, with over 1.4 million attempting suicide every year, much like the number who receive DUIs.

More than 90 percent of people who attempt suicide suffer from depression, have a substance abuse disorder, or both. As I had long experienced but still didn't understand, depression and substance abuse create a vicious cycle. I would use the alcohol to treat anxiety and depression, only to end up more depressed and anxious from the alcohol.

Studies have shown that people who have problems with alcohol have a suicide rate up to 10 times higher than those who do not have problems with alcohol. Forty percent of people who received treatment for a drinking problem report having attempted suicide at least once.

One of the other issues is that when people are drinking, their inhibitions are reduced. It is what allowed me to pursue the affair with Stephen and, ultimately, what made me believe that swallowing a bottle of pills was a good idea while my children slept next door.

Alcohol was destroying everything around me, yet I still couldn't see it. Substance abuse was increasing the severity and duration of my depression, which in turn fueled my suicidal ideations. Not only was alcohol poisoning everything in me; it was also poisoning my marriage, my family—everything I held sacred.

At the hospital they released me with a referral to see a therapist, but I had already been in therapy for years at that point. No one at the hospital asked about my alcohol use, other than to find out what I ingested alongside the pills. Nobody mentioned that maybe drinking was the problem.

On top of that, I had been admitted to the ER just weeks earlier with alcohol poisoning. How obvious did my trail of clues have to be for any of us to discover the culprit?

It was almost like alcohol was too simple a solution. Could that really be all it was?

I felt like my problems had to be so much more severe and complicated than that. It had to be a diagnosis that involved psychiatric disorders, that involved medication, that involved something more than simply quitting drinking.

When we got home, I apologized. I had been sorry a million times before, but, this time, it felt different. We both knew there was only one place lower than the one we were in, and it involved me not coming home from the hospital.

It had shaken both of us up enough to want to make it work.

"I don't know what I would do without you," Kale told me the night after I got home from the hospital. I lay in his arms and finally did the one thing I needed to do since the age of 12: I cried. I cried and cried and cried as I came clean about everything I'd done, apologized for all of it, and committed to doing things differently.

I started texting and calling friends and acquaintances who I'd hurt and started apologizing to them. I called people who I'd lashed out at when I was drunk. I called a new therapist, and Kale and I agreed to go back to marriage counselling. I tried to stay sober that week, showing up for my children and being the wife and mother I once believed myself to be.

But after a few days, I began to convince myself that the attempt was just an accident. I was able to put a new filter on it, thinking that it was just a bad night, not the potentially irreversible trauma for my husband and children it could have been.

I tried to chalk it up the way I did the DUI though I knew far fewer people would commiserate over a suicide attempt.

As much as I tried to normalize the situation, I knew what I'd done wasn't normal. I was a married woman with five kids for God's sake.

I didn't know how to understand my behaviors outside of thinking I was either totally fine or totally beyond saving. And if I was beyond saving, why even try?

The end of alcoholism can feel like you're riding a mechanical bull. There are moments where you're pretty sure you can hang on, when you almost get the rhythm of the bucking bull beneath you. Then, right when you're convinced you've got it, right when you get comfortable in your seat, you get thrown off again.

Over the next week, I would swing wildly from feeling like I had committed an enormous misdeed that needed to be rectified to rationalizing it as a stupid mistake I didn't need to dramatize.

Kale was left in shock. He was the one who had to read that terrible text and call 911. He was the one who would have had to bear the weight of telling our children. Though he had, by default, become the primary parent in the home, that didn't mean he wanted to be the only parent.

"I don't know what we would do without you, Em," he told me the night we came home from the hospital.

This time, I believed him. I knew how important it was that I get better, that I survive.

Still, the very next week, when I went to an event for work, I took a glass of bubbly from a server without thinking twice.

Chapter Twenty-Two: Surrender

I wish I could say that over the next four months, I worked to get better.

But, again, we had enough good moments to fool ourselves into thinking everything was normal. We would get to a place of good enough, and I would once again delay any real change.

That's the tricky thing about rock bottoms: once you're down there, you have nowhere to go but up. The second I was going back to work, spending time with friends, and going to parties with Kale, I believed I was doing better.

Kale's 40th birthday was that winter, and I was planning a huge party for him. Since I had bought him tickets to Oktoberfest in Munich for his birthday, we decided to do an Oktoberfest theme for the party.

Kathryn, one of my friends, joked, "Don't you think you've done enough drinking for one year?"

I remember bristling at the comment even as I ordered kegs of beer and found a sexy German maid costume online. I knew there was no way I was going to be sober for his party.

In a small way, though, the simple concept of being sober was a small step forward.

Just as my own self-destruction felt inevitable at times, there was a new inevitability on the horizon: sobriety.

In the meantime, I kept drinking.

Sometimes Kale would ignore it; other times, he would ask if I was okay. Drinking was the hardest part of our relationship to unravel. It was something we did together since that first night I went to his house and drank with him and his guy friends.

Alcohol was so deeply woven into our relationship that neither of us knew how to remove it. Instead of quitting, we just forged ahead as though everything was fine.

I returned to the social scene, going to work events and attending parties on the weekend. The only difference was that I now Ubered everywhere, leaving that company car in my garage since, most nights, I wouldn't have been able to start it anyway.

I prepared for Kale's party, using it as my big excuse why I couldn't get sober.

A lot of people who have gotten sober share a similar story. They knew the end was coming; they just didn't know how to get there.

According to 2015 statistics, six percent of the US population suffers from alcohol abuse disorder, yet only six percent of that same population seeks treatment. It's estimated that 88,000 people die from alcohol-related causes annually, which makes alcohol the third leading preventable cause of death in the United States.

Perhaps most heartbreaking is the fact that over 10 percent of children grow up in a home with an alcoholic. My children were part of that 10 percent

One thing that always helped me justify my drinking was that I didn't come from a long line of alcoholics. My parents rarely drank. Whenever I Googled, "Am I an alcoholic?" the genetics question always made me feel confident that I did not fit the alcoholic mold. I also felt confident that I wasn't an alcoholic because I had periods of sobriety when I had been pregnant, but this, I later learned, is common for many women with alcoholism.

Now, looking back at myself and my rationalizations, I think Siri should have popped up on my phone during those searches and screamed, "Yes, Emily. You are an alcoholic!"

I knew one person who was in Alcoholics Anonymous, and, some mornings when the hangover was really bad or I couldn't remember parts of the night before, I would consider calling her. I would lie in bed and look at her name in my phone, but it felt like my fingers were paralyzed to actually make the call.

Sometimes I wonder if the biggest challenge in being a stay-at-home mom and getting sober wasn't that I had too much to do but, rather, that I didn't have enough to do.

I could lie in bed all day and lick my wounds. Once Kale and I hired the au pair, there was always someone to help do my job for me. I could keep drinking because the safety net was just that wide, but, as I was learning, the wider the net, the longer the fall.

No matter how many promises I made, I couldn't stop falling.

Grace is a funny thing. We think it shows up at the foot of the hospital bed. We expect to find it in the lonely jail cell. It actually comes when we least expect it.

Finally, Kale's 40th birthday party arrived.

"This is the best party ever," Janie gushed as all our friends showed up in the middle of winter wearing their German costumes, getting drunk on kegs and kegs of beer.

It was like being in college, except most of the attendees were well in their 40s or getting very close.

The holidays were quickly approaching, and I made a silent promise to myself that I would slow down on the drinking. I wasn't willing to say the word "quit" yet, but I wanted to be present for my kids. I wanted to make up for the terrible year we just endured and give them a magical Christmas.

And we did.

We went ice skating and baked cookies. We went sledding and decorated gingerbread houses and volunteered. If I looked back at my Instagram feed at that time, I would probably have thought we were the healthiest, happiest family in Seattle.

There are even photos of me sitting in Kale's lap as we beamed at the camera.

They say a picture can tell a thousand words, but it can also tell a thousand lies.

I don't know what happened, but as soon as Christmas was over, all bets were off.

At the end of December, Kale and I went out with another couple for dinner. I don't remember drinking any more than usual. We split a couple bottles of wine with them before heading home just after midnight. But the next few days would become a blur as I moved in and out of consciousness, swerving from hangover to intoxication.

It was year-end in my business as well, so I was really busy, yet I was on conference calls I didn't remember and spent time with my kids I couldn't recall. I was living in oblivion, and, as I began to realize, people weren't even paying attention anymore.

This wasn't me getting plastered and getting a DUI; this was me getting dinner with friends and being blacked out for days.

I woke up on New Year's Day to the sound of Kale downstairs in the kitchen. I heard him with the kids, parenting, going along without me as if I wasn't needed.

Nothing before—*nothing*—had felt like such a reckoning.

I realized in that moment that I didn't have to kill myself to fade away. Grace wasn't the big bang of my bad behaviors, it was the quiet whisper that said, "You are slowly eliminating yourself."

I could see the future so clearly.

It would just be Kale and the kids, and I would no longer have a role in their lives. I had been sick for so many years, but it was the sound of their laughter, of them living their lives without me, that moved something so deep inside me, I rolled over and called the one sober friend I knew.

Amber answered the phone on the first ring as though she had been waiting for the call.

"I'm so tired," I cried to her, keeping my voice down so Kale didn't hear.

"I know, honey," Amber replied, and I could tell by the tone of her voice that she did.

We agreed to meet at a church in her neighborhood that afternoon. I didn't tell Kale where I was going, just that I was meeting a friend. I don't know if I was ashamed or embarrassed or if I just didn't want to be held accountable if I decided I never wanted to go back.

I drove up to the church where Amber stood waiting for me outside.

I waved dumbly, pulling into a parking space. My hands shook as I walked into the church with her.

I could hear people laughing and chatting with each other as we walked into a small room. I expected everyone to look different. I don't know what I thought a bunch of alcoholics were supposed to look like, but I was surprised to find they looked just like me, just like us.

Normal people.

Though there weren't that many in attendance.

"It's New Years," Amber joked. "Most newcomers don't show up until the third." She nudged me lovingly. "You're early."

It was January 1, 2017 and, for the first time, I finally said the words that had been on the tip of my tongue for nearly 20 years: "I'm Emily, and I'm an alcoholic." The first time I sat down in that faded folding chair, I knew I was home.

I felt far from early, but, as I would soon realize, despite all the terrible things that had happened, despite how painful all the twists and turns were on my marriage, on my family, and on my soul, I was right on time.

Chapter Twenty-Three: Learning How to Heal

The next day, the kids were back in school, but Kale had the day off. We went to lunch, and I told him where I'd gone the day before.

"I am going to stop drinking. For good," I said, tears starting to well up.

"You think that's what you need?" he asked. I know he meant it with the best of intentions. For so long, we both saw drinking as a consequence, not the problem, but I couldn't help but wonder: If I removed the consequence, what would the problem look like?

That day, as I sat in the meeting listening to other people's experiences—not just of their addictions but of their lives—I saw reflections of myself, the kind I had wanted to find. I heard stories of hope, but, more than that, I heard stories being told in a language I could understand.

I didn't want to sound too sure of the process. I think part of me was hoping there was an out—that I could heal and still have a beer while Kale barbequed with our friends.

I just wanted to be a normal woman who could drink...normally. I didn't want to be the weird girl at the party with a seltzer in her hand rather than a marg. But I was at a place in my life where the party was killing me.

"I want to try. I don't know what other choice I have," I offered.

Kale nodded, willing to try anything at this point. "I get it," he said. "I just see that sometimes you drink too much, and sometimes you're able to quit. Can an alcoholic do that?"

At first, I didn't know how to answer that question, but I kept going to those meetings, and I began to relate. The weirdest part was that I felt so much better. It wasn't just that the hangovers were gone. It was like the sky was bluer. Food tasted better. Even the love for my children felt more alive. I was more engaged with everything.

I was more present in my life.

About three months into my sobriety, someone asked the following from the podium: Would you rather stop drinking and not have any consequences or keep trying until you die?

In Alcoholics Anonymous, there is a survey with 20 questions to determine if you're an alcoholic. Though I could say yes to most of them, all I needed was that one question: Would I rather stop drinking and not have any consequences, or did I want to keep trying until I was dead?

Now that I had gotten a taste of the sober life, I realized I didn't want to die.

And the longer I stayed sober, the more I began to heal.

At first, it was hard for Kale. I realized that one of the reasons it had been so difficult for me to quit was because alcohol had become a part of our love language. Life had shoved us together and, instead of really getting to know one another, we used alcohol to lubricate the marriage. We had more fun together when we were drinking, so much that it became the way we related to one another.

Initially, Kale asked if my sobriety meant he needed to quit too, but my sponsor suggested I let him know that was his decision.

I know it wasn't easy for him. I had already made so many demands on our marriage and on him, and now he was being asked to give up his own means of relaxation and entertainment because, yet again, I had a problem.

Over time, however, Kale found his own place with it. He stopped drinking during the week and during family time. Over the years prior, he had joined me whenever I drank, unknowingly enabling my behavior even though that was the last thing he wanted to do. He isn't an alcoholic; he can still go out and have a couple of beers. It doesn't end in affairs or DUIs or suicide attempts. It ends in a couple of beers.

I saw where my own story ended after a couple of beers, and I didn't want to go back there.

There is a tradition of anonymity in Alcoholics Anonymous. We aren't supposed to share our membership in public. Though I am in no way a spokesperson for the program, I didn't want to keep my sobriety private. I wanted people to know where I had been, what I had gone through, and how I had survived. I found that my alcoholism wasn't such a secret after all.

Those first months were exhilarating. I received pats on the back from people in the program, my family, and strangers on the internet, and I started learning more about my disease. I think it is one of the reasons why I have become so open about all my addictions, not just my drinking.

Addiction breeds in secret. My trauma, my eating disorder, my drinking, my affair: the longer I left these things locked up in a dark closet, the bigger and bigger they grew, until they overwhelmed everything.

I had been sober a couple of months when I realized it was time to look at the problem beneath the problem. It was time to start unraveling my trauma, or, more specifically, the diagnosis of unresolved Post Traumatic Stress Disorder (PTSD), which our last therapist offered but I was unable to confront.

Unresolved PTSD leaves your nervous system in a chronic state of overwhelm.

The autonomic nervous system (ANS) plays a significant role in our emotional and physiological responses to stress and trauma. The ANS is understood to have two primary systems: the sympathetic nervous system and the parasympathetic nervous system. The sympathetic nervous system is associated with the fight or flight response and the release of cortisol throughout the bloodstream. The parasympathetic nervous system puts the brakes on the

sympathetic nervous system, so the body stops re-
leasing stress chemicals and shifts toward relaxation
and regeneration. The sympathetic and parasympathetic nervous systems are meant to work together
to support healthy functioning.

When trauma interferes with the rhythmic balance of sympathetic and parasympathetic nervous
system action, there is a breakdown in how the body
responds to stress. In order to heal from PTSD, I had
to begin healing that wound from so many years before.

I started working with an Eye Movement Desen-
sitization and Reprocessing (EMDR) therapist.
EMDR is a psychotherapy that uses eye movements
(or other bilateral stimulation) to help clients process different memories through the same biological
mechanisms involved in Rapid Eye Movement
(REM) sleep. Through this therapy, internal associa-
tions arise and the client begins to process the
memory and disturbing feelings.

Instead of feeling horror and self-disgust around
a traumatic event, we get to translate those feelings
into, "I am strong, and I am safe."

As they say: the wound doesn't close; it just
transforms.

I had spent so many years burying my trauma.
From those early lies in childhood to nearly dying of
suicide in a hospital, I had been unable to live in the
real world. I kept feeling pulled back into the darkness, but, now, I was learning to live in the light.

I had never been able to share these things in my head, but I felt safe sharing my experiences and how those experiences made me feel in AA.

Just as I was finding my own voice, I began to see it emerge all around me. #metoo was just gaining steam, and I saw my story echoed in the voices of so many others.

For the first time I realized I wasn't alone. Tragically, I was in enormous company.

I knew that I needed to tell my story, not to bring further shame to my family but to help other women be released from theirs.

I started talking about my addiction, I started sharing about my anxiety, and I started seeing other women nod their heads, connecting to my truth.

I was so far from alone.

For the first time in my life, I was right in the middle.

Chapter Twenty-Four: Finding Joy

Over the last few years, I have finally moved from the highlight reel to the highlight real. I started sharing where I was at, not just with my friends, but online. I've shared my journey toward recovery as well as my journey to healing my marriage.

At first, it felt like I was high from sobriety, but then I woke up in real life, and a lot of the issues that had plagued Kale and I from before we got married were still there. Prior to getting sober, I had never had a sexual encounter without alcohol. Other than pregnant sex, its own weird experience, I was never sober with any partner at any point. I was starting over in that department and getting sober didn't make it any easier. Essentially, I was learning how to be intimate for the first time with someone I had been married to for almost 15 years. We enlisted the help of a specialized therapist to help me through the unique challenges I faced. It was well worth the work.

Though I felt like I had aged 20 years in six months, my husband was the same supportive, loyal, and loving guy I married. It was hard at first for him to accept how public I was about my journey. He comes from a world of Catholic guilt where you sweep your sins under the rug. On the other hand, I learned that if you keep trying to throw all that shit into the backseat, it will only smack you in the back of the head when you finally hit the brakes.

I had to get it out, and, over time, Kale begin to see that I was being surrounded by an amazing, supportive community. He saw that in sharing our shit, other people were being helped through theirs—and so were we.

It wasn't just in the bedroom that we were getting to know one another. So much of our relationship had been centered around alcohol; it had been about the party since that first night, and, now, it felt like the party was over.

I started taking classes and workshops online, receiving certifications for recovery coaching not to necessarily become a coach but to better understand myself and others. In a workshop called "The Joy in the Journey," I learned that I had to start finding the joy in the challenges of my marriage and of parenthood. Kale and I had to begin finding joy together.

One evening we were at a mini golf place with our kids, and I felt Kale come up behind me. It was probably one of the least romantic places on earth (unless you were a pre-pubescent teen). He murmured in my ear, "There is nobody I would have rather gone through this with."

I can't imagine how anyone would want to go through what I put us through, but I am so glad we didn't give up. I'm so glad Kale didn't give up on me.

Just as our relationship began to change, so did a lot of my friendships. In getting sober, I discovered who my real friends were. Some of them were the women I would have previously considered "mean girls," women I never would have suspected would stick by me through it all. Some were people who initially judged me but softened as they watched my life transform, reaching out to learn more. Some were friends and colleagues who stood by me through thick and thin, never wavering. Others were women I hurt badly during my drinking years, but I made amends to them and forged new relationships in the process.

There were, of course, also some losses. I realized that some friends were only around because they could match my desire to party. Once the party was gone, there was no mutual connection. Many friends fell away for other reasons, even the ones I would have expected to stay.

My circle shrank but became stronger than any shield I ever had before. These were women who wanted to walk through the fire with me, their swords lifted high.

Though most of them continued to drink, some also got sober themselves, seeing the transformation in my life.

Those who continued to drink were often happy when I joined them out for the night.

"I'm so glad you're here," they would tell me. "I won't have to drink either."

Who would have thought?

On my first sober birthday, Kale drove me to the hospital to get my second cervical cancer surgery, which had unfortunately returned that year.

A few months prior, the doctor sat in the office with me, giving me the news, while she explained, "The surgery is going to be more aggressive this time. More time in the hospital, much more downtime. But from what we can tell from your scans, surgery should be all the treatment you'll need."

I was less concerned about the surgery and more about what would happen post-op.

"I'm worried about the painkillers."

My doctor nodded, knowing my history.

"I don't want to take anything I can get high from," I told her. "I'm coming up on a year of sobriety next month, and last time the Vicodin was...a problem."

"Of course; we will do everything we can to make this smooth for you," my doctor kindly assured me. "We have the same goal."

During my first year of sobriety, I had been taking Naltrexone, which prevents the body from experiencing the effects of alcohol. It was an insurance policy. If I did drink, I wouldn't get anything from it. In fact, I would have just gotten terribly sick. Luckily, I never drank or felt the urge to drink, but it helped having that insurance policy in place.

My doctor explained that I would need to come off it for the surgery. As terrified as I was, I was ready to be done with the medication. I was ready to stay sober on my own.

On January 2, 2018, I had a radical hysterectomy. Thankfully, they removed everything, and, afterwards, my doctors worked with me to get through the pain with as little opiate dependency as possible. In fact, I only took them while in the hospital though my husband had a good laugh when I asked him to hit the Taco Bell drive thru the moment I was discharged.

Old habits die hard, especially when drugged!

The small army that had become my circle of friends rallied around me, bringing us dinner, taking care of me, and helping with the kids.

It was a strange way to celebrate my first year sober, but as good friends visited with me, sat beside me, talked about sobriety, healing, and making peace with our pasts, I realized there was nowhere else I would rather be.

Since I was off the Naltrexone, I talked to my doctor about also getting off Wellbutrin. I remained on Zoloft for another year, slowly learning how to better manage anxiety both from within and outside of myself. However, I cannot overstate that I'm a huge believer in medication and would have no problem going back on it if things began to go dark again. It saved my life more than once. I hold my higher power in one hand, and science in the other. Though there are varied opinions on this, I don't believe sober means being 100 percent medication free.

Not long after my surgery, I began transcranial medical stimulation (TMS), which helps stimulate serotonin production in the brain, and continued

EMDR. I saw a therapist weekly. I became focused on healing my brain *and* my body. Then I began to focus on healing my relationships with my children.

I started finding joy in my time with them, trying to make up for all the time I lost.

Prior to getting sober, parenthood had been a suffocating activity that made me feel like I was never doing enough. I felt trapped by my children's needs and demands. After sobriety, I began to see them as people who just wanted to be with me. I began to change my experience of them. Now, when they are climbing all over me or all want something at once, I tell myself, *They love you so much* rather than feel suffocated. I work towards paying attention to their needs as I honor my own.

As my kids start to become teenagers, and I see those little babies slip away, I know how precious the quiet moments are with them. I know I'll miss the chaotic moments too. I know that one day they will be faced with their own choices. Maybe they have this disease in their blood. I know that they watched a lot of things I wished they hadn't. I don't know what their own journeys will look like. All I can do is be honest with my own. I'm honest with them about being sober and about what alcohol did to my life. I grew up keeping secrets. I don't want my kids to live in my own unhealed trauma. I want them to see me heal. I want them to know what healing looks like.

There are still times when mommy needs her own time out, when I have to take a break to take care of me. The difference is that it usually looks like me writing in my journal for a moment, meditating outside, or taking a bath—not self-medicating with a bottle of champagne.

I no longer treat the boundaries in my life like dotted lines, whether that means boundaries with my time, with my family, with my sanity, or with my marriage. I have built concrete walls around the things I wish to keep sacred.

If I have something scheduled with my kids, my colleagues don't have access to that time. If a man flirts with me, I walk away. I am not concerned with being polite. I'd rather be considered a bitch than threaten the people I hold dear. Just because I turn a head doesn't mean I need to respond to it. For a long time, I always believed that I had to respond to other peoples' attention. I believed that I needed to control the interaction between myself and another man by engaging in it. Now I realize that we are able to protect ourselves simply by saying no and walking away. The firmer we are in our boundaries, the less likely people are to cross them.

For so long, I let my addictions (including my addictions to other people and their approval) control my life. Today, I put my sanity and the people I love before those who don't deserve my attention.

That includes the way many moms around me still parent and party.

We live in a world where a mom can't get through a one-hour flag football game without putting out a picnic blanket, popping a bottle, and passing around the solo cups. We are told that mommy needs to drink to enjoy her children.

We live in a world where not drinking is greeted with "Are you pregnant?" or "Are you on antibiotics?" Sobriety is considered a life sentence, not a healthy choice.

We live in a world of over-information, full of scare tactics and fear-based marketing where people overanalyze every ingredient they put on their skin and in their body. We worry about GMOs and corn syrup and gluten, but we're totally fine with mimosas in the morning.

We live in a world where people obsess over what their children look like. We put the focus on the party; whether the booze is at the PTA meeting, on vacation, at the playgroup, or the sporting event, our kids are learning that booze is the answer, no matter the question.

As a 40-year old woman, I can see how much parenting has changed since I was young. Times change, and we grow and learn. Each generation has a different way of doing things.

The ways our parents parented are looked down upon now. It's not that they were all bad, but some of it set us up to fail.

When our parents told us to "Clean your plate!" we learned to ignore our own hunger cues. When little boys were told, "Don't cry" or "Be a man," they learned to stuff their feelings down and become more aggressive. When little girls were told, "Aren't you just the prettiest thing!" or "Look how skinny you are!" we learned our looks were what mattered.

Today, we can sit back and judge all those old ways of parenting, but what does it say about us that we do so with a drink in hand? How has "Do as I say, not as I do" not only escaped us but overwhelmed modern parenting?

The thing is, despite the world we live in, we all have the opportunity to change it. I participated for so long in that drinking culture. I made so many idiotic jokes about using booze to survive motherhood. What does that say to our children about their own worth? That we have to check out to survive them?

Through sobriety, I have discovered that parenthood is a lot more fun and a lot more sacred than we give it credit for. The universe has granted us a brief and important job of guiding these little souls to their own destinies. We can take the job lightly and try to shirk the responsibility, or we can dig in with all the passion and joy it deserves.

For me, getting sober meant getting passionate again—about my marriage, about my children, about my life, and about the world we live in.

And guess what? I've returned to music, some of the best (and cheapest) therapy I have ever received. I play in a local orchestra and sing in a local choir.

After nearly 30 years, I have found the same peace in music I once discovered so long ago. It might have been years since I spoke the language, but I never forgot the tune. The music is pure again.

There have of course been some dark days as well, because life didn't end when I got sober.

Kale and I still get in fights that, at times, make me wonder if we're just too different to make it work. Some nights I lose my temper before bed, feeling just as out of control as when I had a drink in my hand.

But my worst day sober is still far better than my best day drunk.

After my surgery, year two was so much easier. Year three has been easier still. I have seen other people relapse and go back to drinking, and I can feel their sadness. I go to meetings to share hope and remind myself what I don't want to revisit. I know that misery from which you cannot escape, no matter how dark it gets.

There are days when I wonder if this was all I needed all along—if by getting sober, I slayed the dragon in one simple deed.

But I know my story is my story because it was what I needed to learn. As painful as it was for me and my family, it was also in the darkness that I found that glimmer of light.

I learned that I could curate the truth as much as I wanted, but there was nothing as beautiful as the real thing once I removed the filters, and stepped out of the lie and into this bright and brilliant life.

Conclusion

At times, it seems our whole world has become a highlight reel. People offer photoshopped versions of themselves with the mantra, "the prettier the picture, the better the lie."

Life is messy, and #momlife is even messier, but once you look behind the little squares, you begin to realize life isn't as good as the fantasy being projected. Wives cheat, husbands lie, and children throw temper tantrums or struggle with learning disabilities. After getting sober, it was like the big filter under which I lived my life fell away; once I started showing people the truth, they reflected their true lives back on me.

I heard from a mom of three in Florida battling cancer. I heard from a woman in Iowa who just couldn't stop drinking. Every day, I hear from a chorus of people who hold themselves up to an impossible standard then wonder why they are miserable when they can't reach perfection.

Years before, I had a therapist who told me no one was perfect.

It took me nearly 20 years and an enormous amount of imperfection to accept truth. Sure, I messed up, but I was no better or worse than all those other women in their little boxes trying to figure out this little thing called life.

As writer and national treasure, Anne Lamott, once wrote, "Hope begins in the dark, the stubborn hope that if you just show up and try to do the right thing, the dawn will come. You wait and watch and work: you don't give up."

I didn't give up. And neither should you.

Before I type my last words here, I hope you believe that. Wherever you are, whatever you are going through, the trials are always worth it once you get to the other side—whether that's the other side of sobriety, the other side of marriage, or the other side of trauma.

I have seen so many people come to the other side. I have friends who have gotten sober or tackled eating issues. They once lived in secrecy; now they talk openly about their depression or anxiety.

I used to wear t-shirts that said, "Prosecco made me do it." Now I see the drinking mom culture for what it is: a desperate plea for help.

I have done a lot of hard things but none of them compares to motherhood.

Back when women were all in the hut together, raising their children side by side, they had the support needed to be the present parents those times required. Today, we are on our own. We stand in the kitchen screaming by ourselves, and we wonder why no one is listening.

Find the squad that will listen. Hold them close. Walk each other through the hard shit, and tell each other the hard truths.

We can do it alone and wonder why we feel so lonely, or we can do it together.

We can walk in the fellowship of the spirit, no matter what that fellowship looks like.

I hope to meet you there.

Acknowledgements

First and foremost, thank you to my person (and favorite superfood), Kale, for sticking by my side when nobody would have blamed you for leaving. You are my best friend, my favorite human, and the best husband ever. Also, you are the cutest. Thank you for trusting me and supporting me on this journey and every journey—even the ones you thought were crazy. I love you.

Thank you Keegan, Riley, Macy, Lainey, and Rowan. You are the reason I wake up every day and do the hard work of becoming a better human. You are worth every second of every struggle I have ever been through. You are everything I've ever wanted in this life, and while your roads won't always be smooth, I hope you always know that being true to yourself is the best way to live. I'm always proud of you. I love you.

Mom, writing this was hard; telling you my story was hard. I know that reading it was even harder for you. I feel like I understand you so much more, not only since becoming a mom, but through writing this book as well. I hope you feel the same about me. I can't imagine having a better mom, and I love our relationship more and more each day. I love you.

Dad, through writing this book, I've realized how much you've taught me. Even when your lessons were hard, and even when I didn't listen, they made a difference. Thank you for showing me what hard work looks like and for giving me just enough of a temper to not take any shit. I love you.

Jason, my brother, I know we haven't always seen eye to eye, and I still question your Oreo consumption, but you have an important, irreplaceable place in my story and my heart. I love you.

Thank you, Marissa O, for being my original partner in crime while also keeping me out of trouble and loving me when I needed help.

Thank you, Sasha, for supporting and loving me during a season in my life when nobody else knew how to.

Thank you, Krista D., for being a good friend, the supportive sister I never had, and for having a cute brother (well, two cute brothers, but one in particular who I married).

Krista M, I miss you every day on this earth. You meant more to me than you ever knew.

Thank you, Brooke, for always being my sounding board, my best friend, my lifeline, my support system, and my shoulder to cry on. Mother's day date 4EVA.

Thank you, Sarah, for your friendship, support, availability, honesty, abundance, tough love, and for being the best sober date I could ask for.

Thank you, Amy, for bringing me to my first AA meeting and opening the door to recovery.

There are too many more friends to thank, but I'm going to try; thank you Michelle, Meredith, Kate, Emily, Blair, Beth, Melissa, Lindsey, Jenifer, Claire, Claudia, Anna, Cathy, Jodie, AJ, Jee, Shaney, Denise, Diana, Renee, Kelly, Wendy, Dawn, Mary Ann, Delicia, Heather, Nicole, Susie, and so many others.

Thank you to my sober community online. The saying is often true in sobriety: nobody supports you like a social media friend you've never actually met!

Thank you to AA, particularly the women of my LL group, for getting me sober and helping me stay sober. It works if you work it, and we're all worth it!

Thank you to SHE RECOVERS for connecting me to like-minded, supportive women and for spreading the message that we are all recovering from something and that all of our stories matter.

Anna David, thank you for making this book happen, for dealing with my million (probably stupid) questions, and for guiding me on my first book experience and making it seamless. Also, thank you for throwing around F-bombs like commas to make me feel right at home. Launch Pad Publishing rocks!

Lauren Wallett, thank you for answering my other million (probably also stupid) questions and for helping so much with my launch. Also, thank you for having such a fantastic accent.

Kristen McGuiness, thank you for helping me wrap my brain around my own story and helping me arrange it in a way that allowed me to fully heal and, hopefully, will help many others to heal as well. I have enjoyed this process so much; I might even be crazy enough to do it again.

About Emily Lynn Paulson

Emily Lynn Paulson is a writer, Certified Professional Recovery Coach, TEDx Speaker and the Founder of Sober Mom Squad. She has discussed how to end the shame and stigma of mental health and substance use disorders on and in *The Doctors, Parade, Today Parents, The Seattle Times* and *USA Today* as well as on the websites Bustle and The Huffington Post.

Sober since January 2, 2017, Emily's recovery path is focused on ruthless honesty, grace and self-love and she believes that sharing our truth with each other is the best resource of all. Paulson resides in Seattle with her husband and their five children. A contributor to *The Addiction Diaries: Stories of Darkness, Hope and All That Falls In Between*, Emily can be found on Instagram @highlightrealrecovery and on the web at www.highlightreallife.com.